D1131561

Statistics

The Shape of the Data

Grade 4

Also appropriate for Grade 5

Susan Jo Russell
Rebecca B. Corwin
Andee Rubin
Joan Akers

Developed at TERC, Cambridge, Massachusetts

Dale Seymour Publications®
Menlo Park, California

Some of the material in this unit was developed by Susan Jo Russell and Rebecca B. Corwin for *Statistics: The Shape of the Data* (a unit in the series *Used Numbers: Real Data in the Classroom*), © 1989 by Dale Seymour Publications®.

The *Investigations* curriculum was developed at TERC (formerly Technical Education Research Centers) in collaboration with Kent State University and the State University of New York at Buffalo. The work was supported in part by National Science Foundation Grant No. ESI-9050210. TERC is a nonprofit company working to improve mathematics and science education. TERC is located at 2067 Massachusetts Avenue, Cambridge, MA 02140.

**This project was supported, in part,
by the
National Science Foundation**
Opinions expressed are those of the authors
and not necessarily those of the Foundation

Managing Editor: Catherine Anderson
Series Editor: Beverly Cory
Revision Team: Laura Marshall Alavosus, Ellen Harding, Patty Green Holubar, Suzanne Knott, Beverly Hersh Lozoff
ESL Consultant: Nancy Sokol Green
Production/Manufacturing Director: Janet Yearian
Production/Manufacturing Coordinator: Amy Changar, Shannon Miller
Design Manager: Jeff Kelly
Design: Don Taka
Illustrations: Jane McCreary, Carl Yoshihara
Cover: Bay Graphics
Composition: Archetype Book Composition

This book is published by Dale Seymour Publications®, an imprint of Addison Wesley Longman, Inc.

Dale Seymour Publications
2725 Sand Hill Road
Menlo Park, CA 94025
Customer Service: 800-872-1100

**DALE
SEYMOUR
PUBLICATIONS**®

Order number DS43895
ISBN 1-57232-748-0
1 2 3 4 5 6 7 8 9 10-ML-01 00 99 98 97

Printed on Recycled Paper

TERC

INVESTIGATIONS IN NUMBER, DATA, AND SPACE®

Principal Investigator   Susan Jo Russell

Co-Principal Investigator   Cornelia C. Tierney

Director of Research and Evaluation   Jan Mokros

Curriculum Development
Joan Akers
Michael T. Battista
Mary Berle-Carman
Douglas H. Clements
Karen Economopoulos
Ricardo Nemirovsky
Andee Rubin
Susan Jo Russell
Cornelia C. Tierney
Amy Shulman Weinberg

Evaluation and Assessment
Mary Berle-Carman
Abouali Farmanfarmaian
Jan Mokros
Mark Ogonowski
Amy Shulman Weinberg
Tracey Wright
Lisa Yaffee

Teacher Support
Rebecca B. Corwin
Karen Economopoulos
Tracey Wright
Lisa Yaffee

Technology Development
Michael T. Battista
Douglas H. Clements
Julie Sarama Meredith
Andee Rubin

Video Production
David A. Smith

Administration and Production
Amy Catlin
Amy Taber

**Cooperating Classrooms
for This Unit**
Virginia Chalmers
Francine Hiller
Cambridge Public Schools
Cambridge, MA

Dorothy Spahr
Wellesley Public Schools
Wellesley, MA

Reina Huerta
New York City Public Schools
New York, NY

Christine Fuentes
Clark County Public Schools
Georgia

Kathleen O'Connell
Arlington Public Schools
Arlington, MA

Michele de Silva
Boston Public Schools
Boston, MA

Consultants and Advisors
Elizabeth Badger
Deborah Lowenberg Ball
Marilyn Burns
Ann Grady
Joanne M. Gurry
James J. Kaput
Steven Leinwand
Mary M. Lindquist
David S. Moore
John Olive
Leslie P. Steffe
Peter Sullivan
Grayson Wheatley
Virginia Woolley
Ann Zarinnia

Graduate Assistants
Kent State University
Joanne Caniglia
Pam DeLong
Carol King

State University of New York at Buffalo
Rosa Gonzalez
Sue McMillen
Julie Sarama Meredith
Sudha Swaminathan

Revisions and Home Materials
Cathy Miles Grant
Marlene Kliman
Margaret McGaffigan
Megan Murray
Kim O'Neil
Andee Rubin
Susan Jo Russell
Lisa Seyferth
Myriam Steinback
Judy Storeygard
Anna Suarez
Cornelia Tierney
Carol Walker
Tracey Wright

CONTENTS

WHERE TO START

The first-time user of *The Shape of the Data* should read the following:

When you next teach this same unit, you can begin to read more of the background. Each time you present the unit, you will learn more about how your students understand the mathematical ideas.

Investigations in Number, Data, and Space® is a K–5 mathematics curriculum with four major goals:

■ to offer students meaningful mathematical problems

■ to emphasize depth in mathematical thinking rather than superficial exposure to a series of fragmented topics

■ to communicate mathematics content and pedagogy to teachers

■ to substantially expand the pool of mathematically literate students

The *Investigations* curriculum embodies a new approach based on years of research about how children learn mathematics. Each grade level consists of a set of separate units, each offering 2–8 weeks of work. These units of study are presented through investigations that involve students in the exploration of major mathematical ideas.

Approaching the mathematics content through investigations helps students develop flexibility and confidence in approaching problems, fluency in using mathematical skills and tools to solve problems, and proficiency in evaluating their solutions. Students also build a repertoire of ways to communicate about their mathematical thinking, while their enjoyment and appreciation of mathematics grows.

The investigations are carefully designed to invite all students into mathematics—girls and boys, members of diverse cultural, ethnic, and language groups, and students with different strengths and interests. Problem contexts often call on students to share experiences from their family, culture, or community. The curriculum eliminates barriers—such as work in isolation from peers, or emphasis on speed and memorization—that exclude some students from participating successfully in mathematics. The following aspects of the curriculum ensure that all students are included in significant mathematics learning:

■ Students spend time exploring problems in depth.

■ They find more than one solution to many of the problems they work on.

■ They invent their own strategies and approaches, rather than relying on memorized procedures.

■ They choose from a variety of concrete materials and appropriate technology, including calculators, as a natural part of their everyday mathematical work.

■ They express their mathematical thinking through drawing, writing, and talking.

■ They work in a variety of groupings—as a whole class, individually, in pairs, and in small groups.

■ They move around the classroom as they explore the mathematics in their environment and talk with their peers.

While reading and other language activities are typically given a great deal of time and emphasis in elementary classrooms, mathematics often does not get the time it needs. If students are to experience mathematics in depth, they must have enough time to become engaged in real mathematical problems. We believe that a minimum of five hours of mathematics classroom time a week—about an hour a day—is critical at the elementary level. The plan and pacing of the *Investigations* curriculum is based on that belief.

We explain more about the pedagogy and principles that underlie these investigations in Teacher Notes throughout the units. For correlations of the curriculum to the NCTM Standards and further help in using this research-based program for teaching mathematics, see the following books:

■ *Implementing the* Investigations in Number, Data, and Space® *Curriculum*

■ *Beyond Arithmetic: Changing Mathematics in the Elementary Classroom* by Jan Mokros, Susan Jo Russell, and Karen Economopoulos

This book is one of the curriculum units for *Investigations in Number, Data, and Space.* In addition to providing part of a complete mathematics curriculum for your students, this unit offers information to support your own professional development. You, the teacher, are the person who will make this curriculum come alive in the classroom; the book for each unit is your main support system.

Although the curriculum does not include student textbooks, reproducible sheets for student work are provided in the unit and are also available as Student Activity Booklets. Students work actively with objects and experiences in their own environment and with a variety of manipulative materials and technology, rather than with a book of instruction and problems. We strongly recommend use of the overhead projector as a way to present problems, to focus group discussion, and to help students share ideas and strategies.

Ultimately, every teacher will use these investigations in ways that make sense for his or her particular style, the particular group of students, and the constraints and supports of a particular school environment. Each unit offers information and guidance for a wide variety of situations, drawn from our collaborations with many teachers and students over many years. Our goal in this book is to help you, a professional educator, implement this curriculum in a way that will give all your students access to mathematical power.

Investigation Format

The opening two pages of each investigation help you get ready for the work that follows.

What Happens This gives a synopsis of each session or block of sessions.

Mathematical Emphasis This lists the most important ideas and processes students will encounter in this investigation.

What to Plan Ahead of Time These lists alert you to materials to gather, sheets to duplicate, transparencies to make, and anything else you need to do before starting.

INVESTIGATION 1

Introduction to Data Analysis

What Happens

Session 1: How Many Raisins in a Box? Students count the raisins in a sample of small boxes of raisins (one box for each student), record and organize the results, and describe the shape of the data distribution. The line plot is introduced as a useful way to make a first-draft visual representation of a set of data.

Sessions 2 and 3: How Many People in a Family? Students decide how to determine family size for their class, then collect family size data in their classroom. They describe the shape of the distribution of family size for their class and determine typical family size from these data. They compare it with the typical family size in their community.

Mathematical Emphasis

- Making quick sketches of the data to use as working tools during the analysis process
- Describing the shape of the data, moving from noticing individual features of the data ("Two boxes had 33 raisins, three boxes had 34 raisins") to describing the overall shape of the distribution ("Over half of the boxes had between 34 and 37 raisins")
- Defining the way data will be collected
- Summarizing what is typical of a set of data

How many raisins are in your box?

35 36
37   35
    34

INVESTIGATION 1

What to Plan Ahead of Time

Materials

- Small (half-ounce) boxes of raisins, at least 1 per student. Alternative: Small packages of other easily countable things that are packed by weight, such as peanuts (Session 1)
- Unlined paper for making sketch graphs (Sessions 1–3)
- Interlocking cubes or a similar concrete material for representing the data, about 150–200 (Sessions 2–3, optional)
- Overhead projector (Sessions 2–3)
- Blank overhead transparencies and pen (Sessions 2–3)

Other Preparation

- Become familiar with making a line plot. See the **Teacher Note,** Sketch Graphs: Quick to Make, Easy to Read (p. 8) and the **Teacher Note,** Line Plots: A Quick Way to Show the Shape of the Data (p. 9).
- Plan to save the empty raisin boxes (Session 1) and the family data (Sessions 2–3) to use in Investigation 2, Session 5.
- Find out the typical family size for your community. Municipal government offices are usually glad to provide this information over the phone. Typically, the figure will be the mean family size in decimal form (e.g., 3.24). The use of decimals is not recommended for this investigation; "about 3" or "between 3 and 4" is accurate enough. (Sessions 2–3)
- Prepare copies of your class list, 1 per student, for recording data. (Sessions 2–3, optional)
- Duplicate student sheets and teaching resources (located at the end of this unit) as follows. If you have Student Activity Booklets, copy only the item marked with an asterisk.

For Sessions 2–3
Student Sheet 1, How Many Brothers and Sisters? (p. 73): 1 per student (homework)
Family letter* (p. 72): 1 per student. Remember to sign it before copying.

- If you plan to provide folders in which students will save their work for the entire unit, prepare these for distribution during Session 1.

Sessions Within an investigation, the activities are organized by class session, a session being at least a one-hour math class. Sessions are numbered consecutively through an investigation. Often several sessions are grouped together, presenting a block of activities with a single major focus.

When you find a block of sessions presented together—for example, Sessions 1, 2, and 3—read through the entire block first to understand the overall flow and sequence of the activities. Make some preliminary decisions about how you will divide the activities into three sessions for your class, based on what you know about your students. You may need to modify your initial plans as you progress through the activities, and you may want to make notes in the margins of the pages as reminders for the next time you use the unit.

Be sure to read the Session Follow-Up section at the end of the session block to see what homework assignments and extensions are suggested as you make your initial plans.

While you may be used to a curriculum that tells you exactly what each class session should cover, we have found that the teacher is in a better position to make these decisions. Each unit is flexible and may be handled somewhat differently by every teacher. While we provide guidance for how many sessions a particular group of activities is likely to need, we want you to be active in determining an appropriate pace and the best transition points for your class. It is not unusual for a teacher to spend more or less time than is proposed for the activities.

Ten-Minute Math At the beginning of some sessions, you will find Ten-Minute Math activities. These are designed to be used in tandem with the investigations, but not during the math hour. Rather, we hope you will do them whenever you have a spare 10 minutes—maybe before lunch or recess, or at the end of the day.

Ten-Minute Math offers practice in key concepts, but not always those being covered in the unit. For example, in a unit on using data, Ten-Minute Math might revisit geometric activities done earlier in the year. Complete directions for the suggested activities are included at the end of each unit.

Sessions 2 and 3

How Many People in a Family?

What Happens

Students decide how to determine family size for their class, then collect family size data in their classroom. They describe the shape of the distribution of family size for their class and determine typical family size from these data. They compare it with the typical family size in their community. Student work focuses on:

■ defining the way data will be collected
■ making quick sketches of the data
■ describing the shape of the data
■ summarizing what is typical of the data

Ten-Minute Math: Estimation and Number Sense Once or twice in the next few days, use this activity. If your class has completed the Fractions unit, *Different Shapes, Equal Pieces*, you may want to do fraction estimation problems.

Present a problem on the chalkboard or overhead, let's say $1/2 + 3/4$, and ask:

Is the answer more than one or less than one?

Allow students to think about the problem for about a minute, and then have them discuss it. Encourage students to imagine fraction cards, dot paper squares, or other materials they've used to think about fractions.

Encourage students to give reasons for their answers, such as, "I know it's more than one because $3/4$ is bigger than $1/2$ and two $1/2$'s are one."

Ask the same question about other problems, such as

$1/3 + 1/4$ $2/3 + 2/3$ $7/8 + 1/4$ $4/5 + 5/6$

Materials

■ Unlined paper
■ Interlocking cubes (optional)
■ Copies of the class list (optional)
■ Student Sheet 1 (1 per student, homework)
■ Family letter (1 per student)
■ Overhead projector
■ Blank transparencies and pen

Sessions 2 and 3: How Many People in a Family? ■ **13**

Activities The activities include pair and small-group work, individual tasks, and whole-class discussions. In any case, students are seated together, talking and sharing ideas during all work times. Students most often work cooperatively, although each student may record work individually.

Choice Time In some units, some sessions are structured with activity choices. In these cases, students may work simultaneously on different activities focused on the same mathematical ideas. Students choose which activities they want to do, and they cycle through them.

You will need to decide how to set up and introduce these activities and how to let students make their choices. Some teachers present them as station activities, in different parts of the room. Some list the choices on the board as reminders or have students keep their own lists.

Extensions Sometimes in Session Follow-Up, you will find suggested extension activities. These are opportunities for some or all students to explore a topic in greater depth or in a different context. They are not designed for "fast" students; mathematics is a multifaceted discipline, and different students will want to go further in different investigations. Look for and encourage the sparks of interest and enthusiasm you see in your students, and use the extensions to help them pursue these interests.

Excursions Some of the *Investigations* units include excursions—blocks of activities that could be omitted without harming the integrity of the unit. This is one way of dealing with the great depth and variety of elementary mathematics— much more than a class has time to explore in any one year. Excursions give you the flexibility to make different choices from year to year, doing the excursion in one unit this time, and next year trying another excursion.

Tips for the Linguistically Diverse Classroom At strategic points in each unit, you will find concrete suggestions for simple modifications of the teaching strategies to encourage the participation of all students. Many of these tips offer alternative ways to elicit critical thinking from students at varying levels of English proficiency, as well as from other students who find it difficult to verbalize their thinking.

The tips are supported by suggestions for specific vocabulary work to help ensure that all students can participate fully in the investigations. The Preview for the Linguistically Diverse Classroom (p. I-19) lists important words that are assumed as part of the working vocabulary of the unit. Second-language learners will need to become familiar with these words in order to understand the problems and activities they will be doing. These terms can be incorporated into students' second-language work before or during the unit. Activities that can be used to present the words are found in the appendix, Vocabulary Support for Second-Language Learners (p. 69). In addition, ideas for making connections to students' language and cultures, included on the Preview page, help the class explore the unit's concepts from a multicultural perspective.

Materials

A complete list of the materials needed for teaching this unit is found on p. I-16. Some of these materials are available in kits for the *Investigations* curriculum. Individual items can also be purchased from school supply dealers.

Classroom Materials In an active mathematics classroom, certain basic materials should be available at all times: interlocking cubes, pencils, unlined paper, graph paper, calculators, things to count with, and measuring tools. Some activities in this curriculum require scissors and glue sticks or tape. Stick-on notes and large paper are also useful materials throughout.

So that students can independently get what they need at any time, they should know where these materials are kept, how they are stored, and how they are to be returned to the storage area. For example, interlocking cubes are best stored in towers of ten; then, whatever the activity, they should be returned to storage in groups of ten at the end of the hour. You'll find that establishing such routines at the beginning of the year is well worth the time and effort.

Technology Calculators are used throughout *Investigations.* Many of the units recommend that you have at least one calculator for each pair. You will find calculator activities, plus Teacher Notes discussing this important mathematical tool, in an early unit at each grade level. It is assumed that calculators will be readily available for student use.

Computer activities at grade 4 use a software program that was developed especially for the *Investigations* curriculum. The program *Geo-Logo*™ is used for activities in the 2-D Geometry unit, *Sunken Ships and Grid Patterns,* where students explore coordinate graphing systems, the use of negative numbers to represent locations in space, and the properties of geometric figures.

How you use the computer activities depends on the number of computers you have available. Suggestions are offered in the geometry units for how to organize different types of computer environments.

Children's Literature Each unit offers a list of suggested children's literature (p. I-16) that can be used to support the mathematical ideas in the unit. Sometimes an activity is based on a specific children's book, with suggestions for substitutions where practical. While such activities can be adapted and taught without the book, the literature offers a rich introduction and should be used whenever possible.

Student Sheets and Teaching Resources Student recording sheets and other teaching tools needed for both class and homework are provided as reproducible blackline masters at the end of each unit. They are also available as Student Activity Booklets. These booklets contain all the sheets each student will need for individual work, freeing you from extensive copying (although you may need or want to copy the occasional teaching resource on transparency film or card stock, or make extra copies of a student sheet).

We think it's important that students find their own ways of organizing and recording their work. They need to learn how to explain their thinking with both drawings and written words, and how to organize their results so someone else can under-

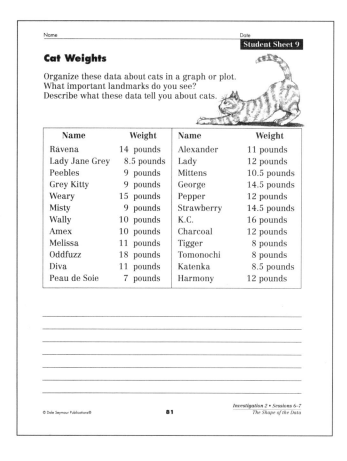

stand them. For this reason, we deliberately do not provide student sheets for every activity. Regardless of the form in which students do their work, we recommend that they keep a mathematics notebook or folder so that their work is always available for reference.

Homework In *Investigations,* homework is an extension of classroom work. Sometimes it offers review and practice of work done in class, sometimes preparation for upcoming activities, and sometimes numerical practice that revisits work in earlier units. Homework plays a role both in supporting students' learning and in helping inform families about the ways in which students in this curriculum work with mathematical ideas.

Depending on your school's homework policies and your own judgment, you may want to assign more homework than is suggested in the units. For this purpose you might use the practice pages, included as blackline masters at the end of this unit, to give students additional work with numbers.

For some homework assignments, you will want to adapt the activity to meet the needs of a variety of students in your class: those with special needs, those ready for more challenge, and second-language learners. You might change the numbers in a problem, make the activity more or less complex, or go through a sample activity with those who need extra help. You can modify any student sheet for either homework or class use. In particular, making numbers in a problem smaller or larger can make the same basic activity appropriate for a wider range of students.

Another issue to consider is how to handle the homework that students bring back to class—how to recognize the work they have done at home without spending too much time on it. Some teachers hold a short group discussion of different approaches to the assignment; others ask students to share and discuss their work with a neighbor, or post the homework around the room and give students time to tour it briefly. If you want to keep track of homework students bring in, be sure it ends up in a designated place.

Investigations at Home It is a good idea to make your policy on homework explicit to both students and their families when you begin teaching with *Investigations*. How frequently will you be assigning homework? When do you expect homework to be completed and brought back to school? What are your goals in assigning homework? How independent should families expect their children to be? What should the parent's or guardian's role be? The more explicit you can be about your expectations, the better the homework experience will be for everyone.

Investigations at Home (a booklet available separately for each unit, to send home with students) gives you a way to communicate with families about the work students are doing in class. This booklet includes a brief description of every session, a list of the mathematics content emphasized in each investigation, and a discussion of each homework assignment to help families more effectively support their children. Whether or not you are using the *Investigations* at Home booklets, we expect you to make your own choices about home-

work assignments. Feel free to omit any and to add extra ones you think are appropriate.

Family Letter A letter that you can send home to students' families is included with the blackline masters for each unit. Families need to be informed about the mathematics work in your classroom; they should be encouraged to participate in and support their children's work. A reminder to send home the letter for each unit appears in one of the early investigations. These letters are also available separately in Spanish, Vietnamese, Cantonese, Hmong, and Cambodian.

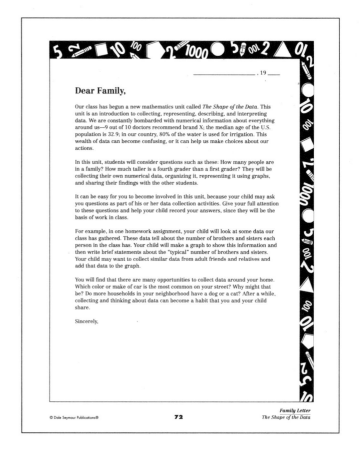

Help for You, the Teacher

Because we believe strongly that a new curriculum must help teachers think in new ways about mathematics and about their students' mathematical thinking processes, we have included a great deal of material to help you learn more about both.

About the Mathematics in This Unit This introductory section (p. I-17) summarizes the critical information about the mathematics you will be teaching. It describes the unit's central mathematical ideas and how students will encounter them through the unit's activities.

Teacher Notes These reference notes provide practical information about the mathematics you are teaching and about our experience with how students learn. Many of the notes were written in response to actual questions from teachers, or to discuss important things we saw happening in the field-test classrooms. Some teachers like to read them all before starting the unit, then review them as they come up in particular investigations.

Dialogue Boxes Sample dialogues demonstrate how students typically express their mathematical ideas, what issues and confusions arise in their thinking, and how some teachers have guided class discussions.

These dialogues are based on the extensive classroom testing of this curriculum; many are word-for-word transcriptions of recorded class discussions. They are not always easy reading; sometimes it may take some effort to unravel what the students are trying to say. But this is the value of these dialogues; they offer good clues to how your students may develop and express their approaches and strategies, helping you prepare for your own class discussions.

Where to Start You may not have time to read everything the first time you use this unit. As a first-time user, you will likely focus on understanding the activities and working them out with your students. Read completely through each investigation before starting to present it. Also read those sections listed in the Contents under the heading Where to Start (p. vi).

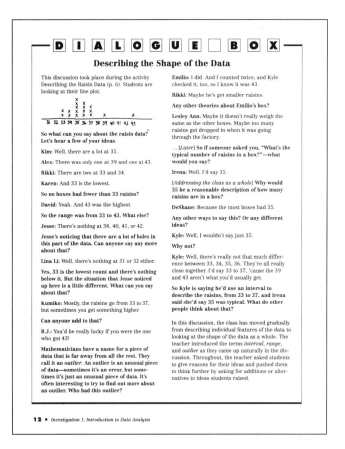

The *Investigations* curriculum incorporates the use of two forms of technology in the classroom: calculators and computers. Calculators are assumed to be standard classroom materials, available for student use in any unit. Computers are explicitly linked to one or more units at each grade level; they are used with the unit on 2-D geometry at each grade, as well as with some of the units on measuring, data, and changes.

Using Calculators

In this curriculum, calculators are considered tools for doing mathematics, similar to pattern blocks or interlocking cubes. Just as with other tools, students must learn both *how* to use calculators correctly and *when* they are appropriate to use. This knowledge is crucial for daily life, as calculators are now a standard way of handling numerical operations, both at work and at home.

Using a calculator correctly is not a simple task; it depends on a good knowledge of the four operations and of the number system, so that students can select suitable calculations and also determine what a reasonable result would be. These skills are the basis of any work with numbers, whether or not a calculator is involved.

Unfortunately, calculators are often seen as tools to check computations with, as if other methods are somehow more fallible. Students need to understand that any computational method can be used to check any other; it's just as easy to make a mistake on the calculator as it is to make a mistake on paper or with mental arithmetic. Throughout this curriculum, we encourage students to solve computation problems in more than one way in order to double-check their accuracy. We present mental arithmetic, paper-and-pencil computation, and calculators as three possible approaches.

In this curriculum we also recognize that, despite their importance, calculators are not always appropriate in mathematics instruction. Like any tools, calculators are useful for some tasks, but not for others. You will need to make decisions about when to allow students access to calculators and when to ask that they solve problems without them, so that they can concentrate on other tools and skills. At times when calculators are or are not appropriate for a particular activity, we make specific recommendations. Help your students develop their own sense of which problems they can tackle with their own reasoning and which ones might be better solved with a combination of their own reasoning and the calculator.

Managing calculators in your classroom so that they are a tool, and not a distraction, requires some planning. When calculators are first introduced, students often want to use them for everything, even problems that can be solved quite simply by other methods. However, once the novelty wears off, students are just as interested in developing their own strategies, especially when these strategies are emphasized and valued in the classroom. Over time, students will come to recognize the ease and value of solving problems mentally, with paper and pencil, or with manipulatives, while also understanding the power of the calculator to facilitate work with larger numbers.

Experience shows that if calculators are available only occasionally, students become excited and distracted when they are permitted to use them. They focus on the tool rather than on the mathematics. In order to learn when calculators are appropriate and when they are not, students must have easy access to them and use them routinely in their work.

If you have a calculator for each student, and if you think your students can accept the responsibility, you might allow them to keep their calculators with the rest of their individual materials, at least for the first few weeks of school. Alternatively, you might store them in boxes on a shelf, number each calculator, and assign a corresponding number to each student. This system can give students a sense of ownership while also helping you keep track of the calculators.

Using Computers

Students can use computers to approach and visualize mathematical situations in new ways. The computer allows students to construct and manipulate geometric shapes, see objects move according to rules they specify, and turn, flip, and repeat a pattern.

This curriculum calls for computers in units where they are a particularly effective tool for learning mathematics content. One unit on 2-D geometry at each of the grades 3–5 includes a core of activities that rely on access to computers, either in the classroom or in a lab. Other units on geometry, measurement, data, and changes include computer activities, but can be taught without them. In these units, however, students' experience is greatly enhanced by computer use.

The following list outlines the recommended use of computers in this curriculum:

Grade 1
Unit: *Survey Questions and Secret Rules* (Collecting and Sorting Data)
Software: Tabletop, Jr.
   Source: Broderbund
Unit: *Quilt Squares and Block Towns* (2-D and 3-D Geometry)
Software: *Shapes*
   Source: provided with the unit

Grade 2
Unit: *Mathematical Thinking at Grade 2* (Introduction)
Software: *Shapes*
   Source: provided with the unit
Unit: *Shapes, Halves, and Symmetry* (Geometry and Fractions)
Software: *Shapes*
   Source: provided with the unit
Unit: *How Long? How Far?* (Measuring)
Software: *Geo-Logo*
   Source: provided with the unit

Grade 3
Unit: *Flips, Turns, and Area* (2-D Geometry)
Software: *Tumbling Tetrominoes*
   Source: provided with the unit

Unit: *Turtle Paths* (2-D Geometry)
Software: *Geo-Logo*
   Source: provided with the unit

Grade 4
Unit: *Sunken Ships and Grid Patterns* (2-D Geometry)
Software: *Geo-Logo*
   Source: provided with the unit

Grade 5
Unit: *Picturing Polygons* (2-D Geometry)
Software: *Geo-Logo*
   Source: provided with the unit
Unit: *Patterns of Change* (Tables and Graphs)
Software: *Trips*
   Source: provided with the unit
Unit: *Data: Kids, Cats, and Ads* (Statistics)
Software: Tabletop, Sr.
   Source: Broderbund

The software provided with the *Investigations* units uses the power of the computer to help students explore mathematical ideas and relationships that cannot be explored in the same way with physical materials. With the *Shapes* (grades 1–2) and *Tumbling Tetrominoes* (grade 3) software, students explore symmetry, pattern, rotation and reflection, area, and characteristics of 2-D shapes. With the *Geo-Logo* software (grades 3–5), students investigate rotations and reflections, coordinate geometry, the properties of 2-D shapes, and angles. The *Trips* software (grade 5) is a mathematical exploration of motion in which students run experiments and interpret data presented in graphs and tables.

We suggest that students work in pairs on the computer; this not only maximizes computer resources but also encourages students to consult, monitor, and teach one another. Generally, more than two students at one computer find it difficult to share. Managing access to computers is an issue for every classroom. The curriculum gives you explicit support for setting up a system. The units are structured on the assumption that you have enough computers for half your students to work on the machines in pairs at one time. If you do not have access to that many computers, suggestions are made for structuring class time to use the unit with five to eight computers, or even with fewer than five.

Assessment plays a critical role in teaching and learning, and it is an integral part of the *Investigations* curriculum. For a teacher using these units, assessment is an ongoing process. You observe students' discussions and explanations of their strategies on a daily basis and examine their work as it evolves. While students are busy recording and representing their work, working on projects, sharing with partners, and playing mathematical games, you have many opportunities to observe their mathematical thinking. What you learn through observation guides your decisions about how to proceed. In any of the units, you will repeatedly consider questions like these:

- Do students come up with their own strategies for solving problems, or do they expect others to tell them what to do? What do their strategies reveal about their mathematical understanding?

- Do students understand that there are different strategies for solving problems? Do they articulate their strategies and try to understand other students' strategies?

- How effectively do students use materials as tools to help with their mathematical work?

- Do students have effective ideas for keeping track of and recording their work? Does keeping track of and recording their work seem difficult for them?

You will need to develop a comfortable and efficient system for recording and keeping track of your observations. Some teachers keep a clipboard handy and jot notes on a class list or on adhesive labels that are later transferred to student files. Others keep loose-leaf notebooks with a page for each student and make weekly notes about what they have observed in class.

Assessment Tools in the Unit

With the activities in each unit, you will find questions to guide your thinking while observing the students at work. You will also find two built-in assessment tools: Teacher Checkpoints and embedded Assessment activities.

Teacher Checkpoints The designated Teacher Checkpoints in each unit offer a time to "check in" with individual students, watch them at work, and ask questions that illuminate how they are thinking.

At first it may be hard to know what to look for, hard to know what kinds of questions to ask. Students may be reluctant to talk; they may not be accustomed to having the teacher ask them about their work, or they may not know how to explain their thinking. Two important ingredients of this process are asking students open-ended questions about their work and showing genuine interest in how they are approaching the task. When students see that you are interested in their thinking and are counting on them to come up with their own ways of solving problems, they may surprise you with the depth of their understanding.

Teacher Checkpoints also give you the chance to pause in the teaching sequence and reflect on how your class is doing overall. Think about whether you need to adjust your pacing: Are most students fluent with strategies for solving a particular kind of problem? Are they just starting to formulate good strategies? Or are they still struggling with how to start? Depending on what you see as the students work, you may want to spend more time on similar problems, change some of the problems to use smaller numbers, move quickly to more challenging material, modify subsequent activities for some students, work on particular ideas with a small group, or pair students who have good strategies with those who are having more difficulty.

Embedded Assessment Activities Assessment activities embedded in each unit will help you examine specific pieces of student work, figure out what it means, and provide feedback. From the students' point of view, these assessment activities are no different from any others. Each is a learning experience in and of itself, as well as an opportunity for you to gather evidence about students' mathematical understanding.

The embedded assessment activities sometimes involve writing and reflecting; at other times, a discussion or brief interaction between student and teacher; and in still other instances, the creation and explanation of a product. In most cases, the assessments require that students *show* what they did, *write* or *talk* about it, or do both. Having to explain how they worked through a problem helps students be more focused and clear in their mathematical thinking. It also helps them realize that doing mathematics is a process that may involve tentative starts, revising one's approach, taking different paths, and working through ideas.

Teachers often find the hardest part of assessment to be interpreting their students' work. We provide guidelines to help with that interpretation. If you have used a process approach to teaching writing, the assessment in *Investigations* will seem familiar. For many of the assessment activities, a Teacher Note provides examples of student work and a commentary on what it indicates about student thinking.

Documentation of Student Growth

To form an overall picture of mathematical progress, it is important to document each student's work in journals, notebooks, or portfolios. The choice is largely a matter of personal preference; some teachers have students keep a notebook or folder for each unit, while others prefer one mathematics notebook, or a portfolio of selected work for the entire year. The final activity in each *Investigations* unit, called Choosing Student Work to Save, helps you and the students select representative samples for a record of their work.

This kind of regular documentation helps you synthesize information about each student as a mathematical learner. From different pieces of evidence, you can put together the big picture. This synthesis will be invaluable in thinking about where to go next with a particular child, deciding where more work is needed, or explaining to parents (or other teachers) how a child is doing.

If you use portfolios, you need to collect a good balance of work, yet avoid being swamped with an overwhelming amount of paper. Following are some tips for effective portfolios:

- Collect a representative sample of work, including some pieces that students themselves select for inclusion in the portfolio. There should be just a few pieces for each unit, showing different kinds of work—some assignments that involve writing, as well as some that do not.

- If students do not date their work, do so yourself so that you can reconstruct the order in which pieces were done.

- Include your reflections on the work. When you are looking back over the whole year, such comments are reminders of what seemed especially interesting about a particular piece; they can also be helpful to other teachers and to parents. Older students should be encouraged to write their own reflections about their work.

Assessment Overview

There are two places to turn for a preview of the assessment opportunities in each *Investigations* unit. The Assessment Resources column in the unit Overview Chart (pp. I-13–I-15) identifies the Teacher Checkpoints and Assessment activities embedded in each investigation, guidelines for observing the students that appear within classroom activities, and any Teacher Notes and Dialogue Boxes that explain what to look for and what types of student responses you might expect to see in your classroom. Additionally, the section About the Assessment in This Unit (p. I-18) gives you a detailed list of questions for each investigation, keyed to the mathematical emphases, to help you observe student growth.

Depending on your situation, you may want to provide additional assessment opportunities. Most of the investigations lend themselves to more frequent assessment, simply by having students do more writing and recording while they are working.

The Shape of the Data

Content of This Unit   This unit provides students with some tools to record, represent, and analyze simple data sets about familiar situations. Students define issues and questions about data they collect. They organize data in rough draft and presentation graphs and look at the shape of the data—the patterns and special features—identifying places where there is a concentration of data (clumps) or where there are no data (holes). Students describe what seems to be typical for a set of data.

Connections with Other Units   If you are doing the full-year *Investigations* curriculum in the suggested sequence for grade 4, this is the sixth of eleven units. Most fourth graders will have the prerequisite measuring skills (as introduced in the third grade unit *From Paces to Feet*), but if they have had little experience with linear measurement, you may want to add an extra day or two at the beginning of Investigation 2 to give them extra practice measuring lengths, such as their height.

This unit can also be used as an introduction to statistics for fifth graders or even older students. The work in this unit is continued in the Data and Fractions unit, *Three out of Four Like Spaghetti*.

Investigations Curriculum ■ Suggested Grade 4 Sequence

Mathematical Thinking at Grade 4 (Introduction)

Arrays and Shares (Multiplication and Division)

Seeing Solids and Silhouettes (3-D Geometry)

Landmarks in the Thousands (The Number System)

Different Shapes, Equal Pieces (Fractions)

▶ *The Shape of the Data* (Statistics)

Money, Miles, and Large Numbers (Addition and Subtraction)

Changes Over Time (Graphs)

Packages and Groups (Multiplication and Division)

Sunken Ships and Grid Patterns (2-D Geometry)

Three out of Four Like Spaghetti (Data and Fractions)

Investigation 1 ▪ Introduction to Data Analysis

Class Sessions	Activities	Pacing
Session 1 (p. 4) HOW MANY RAISINS IN A BOX?	Getting Acquainted with Statistics Estimating the Number of Raisins Collecting, Recording, and Organizing the Data Describing the Raisin Data Extension: Counting Other Groups Extension: Adding Data	minimum 1 hr
Sessions 2 and 3 (p. 13) HOW MANY PEOPLE IN A FAMILY?	How to Count Who's in Your Family What's the Shape of These Data? How Many Brothers and Sisters? Homework: How Many Brothers and Sisters? Extension: Adding More Family Data Extension: Census Data	minimum 2 hr

◑ **Ten-Minute Math** ▪ **Estimation and Number Sense**

Mathematical Emphasis	**Assessment Resources**	**Materials**
▪ Making quick sketches of the data to use as working tools during the analysis process ▪ Describing the shape of the data, moving from noticing individual features of the data to describing the overall shape of the distribution ▪ Defining the way data will be collected ▪ Summarizing what is typical of a set of data	Sketch Graphs: Quick to Make, Easy to Read (Teacher Note, p. 8) The Shape of the Data: Clumps, Bumps, and Holes (Teacher Note, p. 10) Describing the Shape of the Data (Dialogue Box, p. 12) Summarizing Data: What's Typical? (Teacher Note, p. 19)	Small boxes of raisins Unlined paper Concrete materials for representing data (optional) Overhead projector and transparencies Student Sheet 1 Family letter

Investigation 2 ■ Landmarks in the Data

Class Sessions	Activities	Pacing
Session 1 (p. 22) HOW TALL ARE FOURTH GRADERS?	Teacher Checkpoint: Line Plots and What's Typical Measuring Heights in This Class Describing the Class Height Data Comparing Our Class with Other Fourth Grades Homework: How Tall Are Fourth Graders?	minimum 1 hr
Sessions 2 and 3 (p. 28) FOURTH AND FIRST GRADERS: HOW MUCH TALLER?	Measuring First Graders' Heights Comparing Two Sets of Data Publishing Findings	minimum 2 hr
Session 4 (p. 33) LOOKING AT MYSTERY DATA	Describing Mystery Data A Teacher Checkpoint: Mystery Data B and C Homework: Looking at Mystery Data	minimum 1 hr
Session 5 (p. 39) FINDING THE MEDIAN	Finding the Median Height for This Class What's the Median Height of the All-Stars? Homework: How Many Cavities?	minimum 1 hr
Sessions 6 and 7 (p. 45) USING LANDMARKS IN DATA	Organizing Data and Finding the Median Another Mystery Data Set Assessment: Who Has More Cavities?	minimum 2 hr

◔ **Ten-Minute Math** ■ **Estimation and Number Sense, Broken Calculator**

Mathematical Emphasis

- Inventing ways to compare and represent two sets of data by describing the shape of the data and what's typical of the data

- Finding the median in a set of data arranged in numerical order (e.g., when students line up in order by height)

- Finding the median in a set of data grouped by frequency (e.g., on a line plot or other graph)

- Using the median to describe a set of data and to compare one data set to another

Assessment Resources

Teacher Checkpoint: Line Plots and What's Typical (p. 23)

Measuring Heights: Using Tools (Teacher Note, p. 26)

Discussing Invented Methods for Finding Typical Values (Dialogue Box, p. 27)

How Can We Compare Our Class with a First Grade Class? (Dialogue Box, p. 32)

Teacher Checkpoint: Mystery Data B and C (p. 34)

Visualizing Measurement Data (Dialogue Box, p. 38)

What Good Is Knowing the Median? (Dialogue Box, p. 44)

Assessment: Who Has More Cavities? (p. 46)

Common Misconceptions About the Median . . . and How to Help (Dialogue Box, p. 47)

How Many Cavities Do We Have? (Dialogue Box, p. 48)

Materials

Chart paper (optional)

Unlined paper

Measuring tools

Calculators

Art materials for making presentation graphs

Overhead projector

Concrete materials for representing data (optional)

Student Sheets 2–11

Teaching resource sheets

Investigation 3 ■ A Data Project: Investigating Sleep

Class Sessions	Activities	Pacing
Sessions 1 and 2 (p. 52) WHAT DO WE WANT TO FIND OUT?	How Long Do People Sleep? Choosing a Question Working with Preliminary Data Homework: Three Nights' Sleep	minimum 2 hr
Sessions 3, 4, and 5 (p. 59) THE RESEARCH TEAM AT WORK	Collecting, Organizing, and Describing Data Developing Theories and Publishing Findings Assessment: Group Presentations Choosing Student Work to Save Homework: Wake Up! Homework: Representing How People Wake Up	minimum 3 hr

◗ Ten-Minute Math ■ Broken Calculator

Mathematical Emphasis

- Undertaking a complete data analysis project, from defining a question to publishing results

- Carrying out all the stages of a data analysis investigation

- Choosing and refining a research question

- Viewing the data in several different ways, using quick sketches and other representations to organize and display the data

Assessment Resources

I Wanna Do It Myself! (Teacher Note, p. 57)

Helping Students Refine Their Questions (Dialogue Box, p. 58)

Assessment: Group Presentations (p. 60)

Choosing Student Work to Save (p. 61)

Assessment: Group Presentations (Teacher Note, p. 62)

Materials

Materials for making initial representations of data

Overhead projector

Art materials for "publishing" results

Student Sheets 12–14

Teaching resource sheets

Following are the basic materials needed for the activities in this unit. Many of the items can be purchased from the publisher, either individually or in the Teacher Resource Package and the Student Materials Kit for grade 4. Detailed information is available on the *Investigations* order form. To obtain this form, call toll-free 1-800-872-1100 and ask for a Dale Seymour customer service representative.

Small (half-ounce) boxes of raisins: at least 1 per student. (Or, use small packages of other easily countable things that are packed by weight, such as peanuts.)

Interlocking cubes, counting chips, or other concrete material for representing the data: about 150–200 (optional)

Measuring tools—yardsticks, metersticks, or tape measures—1 per group of students

Chart paper for recording data (optional)

Unlined paper for making sketch graphs

Materials for making presentation graphs—a variety of paper including one-inch or one-centimeter graph paper, colored markers or crayons, scissors, glue

Calculators

Overhead projector

The following materials are provided at the end of this unit as blackline masters. A Student Activity Booklet containing all student sheets and teaching resources needed for individual work is available.

Family Letter (p. 72)

Student Sheets 1–14 (p. 73)

Teaching Resources:

   '93 All-Star Cards (p. 84)

   Sleep Table (p. 90)

   One-Centimeter Graph Paper (p. 91)

Practice Pages (p. 93)

Related Children's Literature

Anno, Mitsumasa. *Anno's Magic Seeds.* New York: Philomel Books, 1995.

Rylant, Cynthia. *The Relatives Came.* New York: Bradbury Press, 1985.

Winthrop, Elizabeth. *Shoes.* New York: Harper and Row, 1986.

A Note on Measuring Tools For measuring student heights in Investigation 2, Session 1, you may decide to use either metric or U.S. Standard units. Tape measures calibrated in either centimeter or inches are very useful here.

Some schools may have a combination measuring tool—metersticks that are 100 centimeters long, but that are also calibrated in inches on the reverse. These are fine for use with metric measure; however, be careful if you plan to use them for measuring in inches. They look like yardsticks, but they are actually a little more than 39 inches long. This can be confusing to students (and adults) who use this tool, expecting to measure things in 3-foot lengths.

To reduce the confusion, try covering the extra 3 inches with masking tape when students need yardsticks. When you distribute these tools, explain why you have covered the end. If you can get separate yardsticks and metersticks, use these instead of the combination stick.

People construct much of their knowledge of the world through informal analysis of data they encounter. When we decide that 10:00 P.M. is too late to call a friend, we are basing our actions on data we have noted in the course of our daily lives—that is, most of our friends go to bed around 10, and don't like to be bothered just as they are going to bed. When we decide to make two dozen brownies for a party for six people, it's because we've seen people eat as many as four brownies at a time. Every day, we collect and analyze data in informal ways. Children are no exception. They notice patterns in such data as people's heights, the sizes of pets, and the number of students present in class each day.

The ability to analyze data critically is becoming a prerequisite of democratic life and productive work in the late twentieth century. Unfortunately, these skills have been almost completely absent from schools until the last decade or so. In that time, we have learned that elementary school students can easily work with basic statistical ideas and that they are enthusiastic about collecting and understanding data. The mathematics of data connect to their natural curiosity about the world around them.

This unit presents just a few critical concepts about data, yet those concepts are the basis of practically all statistical thinking. Being able to describe and compare the patterns and special features of data—the shape of the data—is what statistics is really all about. Looking at the way data are distributed provides the basis for interpreting the data as a whole. This unit gives students an introduction to the following processes:

- asking good statistical questions
- recording and organizing collected data
- drawing quick graphs to get a sense of the data
- drawing more precise graphs to look at details of the data
- finding landmarks in the data, including the median
- considering how to describe the "typical" person/measurement in a data set

Working with data provides opportunities for students to use a variety of mathematical skills. For example, talking about the range of a data set and the existence of outliers is related to an understanding of the base ten system. Figuring out the median of a data set involves some counting and division (There are 37 data points; which is the middle one?) as well as more abstract thinking to consider what the median actually says about a data set. The computation students do in data analysis is purposeful, and the analysis they do helps them to understand how mathematics can function as a significant tool for describing, comparing, predicting, and making decisions.

Mathematical Emphasis At the beginning of each investigation, the Mathematical Emphasis section tells you what is most important for students to learn about during that investigation. Many of these mathematical understandings and processes are difficult and complex. Students gradually learn more and more about each idea over many years of schooling. Individual students will begin and end the unit with different levels of knowledge and skill, but all will gain greater knowledge about how we collect, represent, describe, and interpret data from the real world.

Throughout the *Investigations* curriculum, there are many opportunities for ongoing daily assessment as you observe, listen to, and interact with students at work. In this unit, you will find two Teacher Checkpoints:

Investigation 2, Session 1:
Line Plots and What's Typical (p. 23)

Investigation 2, Session 4:
Mystery Data B and C (p. 34)

This unit also has two embedded assessment activities:

Investigation 2, Sessions 6–7:
Who Has More Cavities? (p. 46)

Investigation 3, Sessions 3–5:
Group Presentations (p. 60)

In addition, you can use almost any activity in this unit to assess your students' needs and strengths. Listed below are questions to help you focus your observations in each investigation. You may want to keep track of your observations for each student to help you plan your curriculum and monitor students' growth. Suggestions for documenting student growth can be found in the section About Assessment (p. I-10).

Investigation 1: Introduction to Data Analysis

■ What kinds of quick sketches of the data do students make to use as working tools during the analysis process? Do these give a clear picture of the shape of the data?

■ How do students describe the shape of the data? Do they notice patterns and trends in the data, or do they look only at individual numbers in a data set? How do they describe where most of the data are, where there are no data, and where there are isolated pieces of data?

■ What approaches do students use to summarize data? Do their ways of determining what is "typical" reflect a growing understanding of the center of the data?

Investigation 2: Landmarks in the Data

■ What ways do students come up with to compare and represent two sets of data? Do they describe the shape of the data and what's typical of the data?

■ What inventive and creative ways have students found to construct their presentation graphs? Do these presentations give an organized, clear, and accessible display of the data? Do they support what students have found in their analyses by directing attention to important features of the data?

■ Are students able to find the median in a set of data arranged in numerical order (e.g., when students line up in order by height)?

■ Are students able to find the median in a set of data grouped by frequency (e.g., on a line plot or other graph)?

■ Are students able to use the median and other landmarks in the data to describe a set of data and to compare one data set to another?

Investigation 3: A Data Project: Investigating Sleep

■ How do students go about planning and completing a full data analysis investigation, from deciding the question to creating the final report?

■ How do students choose and refine a research question?

■ How do students collect and display data?

■ How valid are students' conclusions? How comprehensive is their report? Are they able to critique their own investigation (e.g., relationship to other ideas in the unit, limitations of the study, aspects of the research that they might do differently next time, questions they might ask)?

■ Are students able to make sense of different representations for organizing and displaying data?

In the *Investigations* curriculum, mathematical vocabulary is introduced naturally during the activities. We don't ask students to learn definitions of new terms; rather, they come to understand such words as *factor* or *area* or *symmetry* by hearing them used frequently in discussion as they investigate new concepts. This approach is compatible with current theories of second-language acquisition, which emphasize the use of new vocabulary in meaningful contexts while students are actively involved with objects, pictures, and physical movement.

Listed below are some key words used in this unit that will not be new to most English speakers at this age level, but may be unfamiliar to students with limited English proficiency. You will want to spend additional time working on these words with your students who are learning English. If your students are working with a second-language teacher, you might enlist your colleague's aid in familiarizing students with these words, before and during this unit. In the classroom, look for opportunities for students to hear and use these words. Activities you can use to present the words are given in the appendix, Vocabulary Support for Second-Language Learners (p. 69).

height, tall Students measure their own and younger children's *heights*, comparing the results and determining how *tall* typical fourth graders and first graders are; they also use height data in other activities.

pounds, weigh Students will use these terms in analyzing data that report the weights of domestic cats and lions in zoos.

family, people, children (kids) Students collect data on the size of families, and must first decide which people to count as part of "a family."

sleep, time These terms are a key part of the culminating project—an open-ended investigation involving how much time people spend sleeping each day, based on their bedtimes and wake-up times.

In addition to these key words, students will encounter terms related to dental work *(cavities, teeth, dentist)*. Familiarity with these words will be helpful as they work on the assessment activity in Investigation 2, Who Has More Cavities?

Multicultural Extensions for All Students

Whenever possible, encourage students to share words, objects, customs, or any aspects of daily life from their cultures and backgrounds that are relevant to the activities in this unit. For example:

- In Investigation 1, when counting raisins in small snack-size boxes, let students suggest other snack items familiar to them, sold in small packages, that could be similarly counted.

- When the students are discussing family size later in Investigation 1, they might bring in family photos to post. Ask for the words that define the members of a family in the cultures represented in your classroom. Encourage the class to compare and learn the words in different languages for *mother, father, brother, sister*.

Investigations

Introduction to Data Analysis

What Happens

Session 1: How Many Raisins in a Box?
Students count the raisins in a sample of small boxes of raisins (one box for each student), record and organize the results, and describe the shape of the data distribution. The line plot is introduced as a useful way to make a first-draft visual representation of a set of data.

Sessions 2 and 3: How Many People in a Family? Students decide how to determine family size for their class, then collect family size data in their classroom. They describe the shape of the distribution of family size for their class and determine typical family size from these data. They compare it with the typical family size in their community.

Mathematical Emphasis

■ Making quick sketches of the data to use as working tools during the analysis process

■ Describing the shape of the data, moving from noticing individual features of the data ("Two boxes had 33 raisins, three boxes had 34 raisins") to describing the overall shape of the distribution ("Over half of the boxes had between 34 and 37 raisins")

■ Defining the way data will be collected

■ Summarizing what is typical of a set of data

How many raisins are in your box?

35   36

37   35

34

What to Plan Ahead of Time

Materials

- Small (half-ounce) boxes of raisins, at least 1 per student. Alternative: Small packages of other easily countable things that are packed by weight, such as peanuts (Session 1)

- Unlined paper for making sketch graphs (Sessions 1–3)

- Interlocking cubes or a similar concrete material for representing the data, about 150–200 (Sessions 2–3, optional)

- Overhead projector (Sessions 2–3)

- Blank overhead transparencies and pen (Sessions 2–3)

Other Preparation

- Become familiar with making a line plot. See the **Teacher Note,** Sketch Graphs: Quick to Make, Easy to Read (p. 8) and the **Teacher Note,** Line Plots: A Quick Way to Show the Shape of the Data (p. 9).

- Plan to save the empty raisin boxes (Session 1) and the family data (Sessions 2–3) to use in Investigation 2, Session 5.

- Find out the typical family size for your community. Municipal government offices are usually glad to provide this information over the phone. Typically, the figure will be the mean family size in decimal form (e.g., 3.24). The use of decimals is not recommended for this investigation; "about 3" or "between 3 and 4" is accurate enough. (Sessions 2–3)

- Prepare copies of your class list, 1 per student, for recording data. (Sessions 2–3, optional)

- Duplicate student sheets and teaching resources (located at the end of this unit) as follows. If you have Student Activity Booklets, copy only the item marked with an asterisk.

For Sessions 2–3

Student Sheet 1, How Many Brothers and Sisters? (p. 73): 1 per student (homework)

Family letter* (p. 72): 1 per student. Remember to sign it before copying.

- If you plan to provide folders in which students will save their work for the entire unit, prepare these for distribution during Session 1.

How Many Raisins in a Box?

Materials

- Half-ounce boxes of raisins (1 per student)
- Unlined paper

What Happens

Students count the raisins in a sample of small boxes of raisins (one box for each student), record and organize the results, and describe the shape of the data distribution. The line plot is introduced as a useful way to make a first-draft visual representation of a set of data. Student work focuses on:

- recording the collected data
- organizing the data
- sketching a graph of the data
- examining the shape of the data

Activity

Getting Acquainted with Statistics

This year, as part of our mathematics work, we will be studying statistics. Have you ever heard the word *statistics*? Can you give me any examples of statistics?

Students may know about the use of statistics in sports or in opinion polls.

Statistics is the study of data. Data give us information about something in the real world. We can collect some data right now. How many people in this room have a pet (have brown eyes, speak Spanish, once lived in a different country, take the bus to school)?

Ask several of these questions, count the student responses, and point out that these are data (for example, "Our data show that 12 students in this class take the bus to school").

People collect data by counting, as we just did, or by measuring or by doing experiments. Who can think of some data we can collect by measuring?

Students may think of examples such as the size of the classroom, their heights, or the distance from home to school. Encourage them to think of measures involving weight, volume, time, or temperature, as well.

After mathematicians or scientists have collected their data, they study the data carefully and look for patterns that could tell them something important. For example, data about traffic accidents might give information about which kinds of cars are the safest or whether seat belts make a difference. Data about the number of fish in certain lakes or rivers could give clues about the effects of water pollution.

If possible, provide an example of the use of statistics in your school or community. For example, in one school, a particular piece of playground equipment was forbidden to students younger than fourth grade. The principal used data about injuries on this piece of equipment to make a decision about who could use it. Many of the younger students, it turned out, did not have big enough hands to grasp the bars securely.

Just like mathematicians and scientists who use statistics, we can collect data to find out information about ourselves or the world around us. Today, we are going to start by collecting data about something familiar—a box of raisins.

Estimating the Number of Raisins

Give a box of raisins to each student. Ask students to keep the boxes closed.

Does anybody have an idea about how many raisins there are in a box this size?

Let students offer their ideas. Some may think that because the boxes have the same weight, they have the same number of raisins. Some may think that it would be too hard to put the same number in each box. Have students open their boxes so they can see the top layer of raisins.

What do you think now? Do you want to revise your estimate?

Allow enough time for students to discuss all their ideas. Then pose follow-up questions, for example:

Why do you think there will be about 50? Your idea is very different from Luisa's; how did each of you arrive at your estimate? Will the number of raisins in each box be the same or different? Why do you think so?

Collecting, Recording, and Organizing the Data

Students open their boxes and count the raisins. As they finish their counts, they report their data. Record the numbers in a list on the chalkboard, in whatever order they are reported.

If we wanted to organize these data better, what could we do?

Take a few suggestions from the students. Then have them work in pairs or groups of three, each group choosing one way to organize the data quickly and making a sketch to show it. Emphasize that this is a rough draft sketch; it need not be done meticulously. Once students have organized the data, each group should write down three important things they can say about their data.

Ask a few students to demonstrate their methods for organizing the data, or quickly demonstrate them yourself on the board. Make sure that all the types of representation students have invented are demonstrated. See the **Teacher Note,** Sketch Graphs: Quick to Make, Easy to Read (p. 8).

Mathematicians have invented ways of showing data, too. Here's one way that's easy to use. It's called a *line plot*.

Organize the raisin data on a line plot large enough for everyone to see. For explanation and an example, see the **Teacher Note,** Line Plots: A Quick Way to Show the Shape of the Data (p. 9).

Describing the Raisin Data

What are some of the things you wrote down about these data?

Help students express their initial ideas. To help them get started on this complex question, see the **Teacher Note,** The Shape of the Data: Clumps, Bumps, and Holes (p. 10). The **Teacher Note,** Range and Outliers (p. 11), talks about terms useful in discussing data.

❖ **Tip for the Linguistically Diverse Classroom** Encourage students with limited English proficiency to come up and point to the line plot, using gestures and single words to communicate what they notice about the shape of the data, as you help them verbalize their ideas.

What else can you say about these data? Does anyone have another way to describe this representation? Suppose someone asked you, "About how many raisins are in a box?" What could you say?

See the **Dialogue Box,** Describing the Shape of the Data (p. 12), for a sample discussion.

Making Predictions Ask students to speculate about what adding new information would do to the shape of the data.

If we opened five more boxes of raisins, what is your best guess about how many raisins would be in them, based on the data we already have?

Students work on this question for a few minutes in small groups, then report their theories back to the whole class. Expect them to give reasons for their ideas. Encourage students to ask each other questions and to discuss reasons for the differences among their ideas.

At the end of the session, have each student write inside the top flap the number of raisins found in that box. Then allow students to eat the raisins. Collect and save the boxes for use as a data set in Investigation 2 of this unit.

Session 1 Follow-Up

Counting Other Groups Try a similar activity with other materials—packages of peanuts, packages of sunflower seeds, or fresh peas in pods. What is the shape of the data this time? Is it harder or easier to predict how many will be in a new package?

Adding Data Students are very interested in what happens when they add to their data. Have students count the raisins in extra boxes and add their findings to the class data. Or, keep the class data posted and add to them periodically. Do these additional data change the shape of the data distribution in any way? You could use the raisin boxes themselves to make a more permanent display.

 **Extensions**

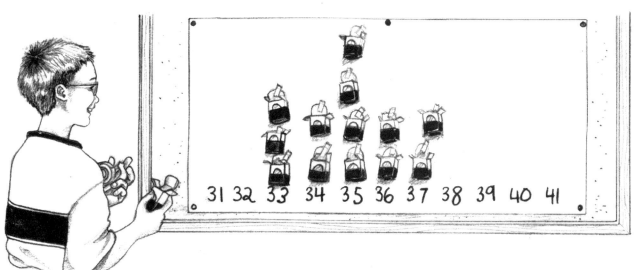

Sketch Graphs: Quick to Make, Easy to Read

Graphing is often taught as an art of presentation, the end point of the data analysis process, the means for communicating what has been found. Certainly, a pictorial representation is an effective way to present data to an audience at the end of an investigation. But graphs, tables, diagrams, and charts are also data analysis tools. A user of statistics employs pictures and graphs frequently during the process of analysis in order to better understand the data.

Many working graphs need never be shown to anyone else. Students can make and use them just to help uncover the story of the data. We call such representations *sketch graphs* or *rough draft graphs*.

We want students to become comfortable with a variety of such working graphs. Sketch graphs should be easy to make and easy to read; they should not challenge students' patience or fine motor skills. Unlike graphs for presentation, sketch graphs do not require neatness, careful measurement or scaling, use of clear titles or labels, or decorative work.

Sketch graphs:

- can be made rapidly
- reveal aspects of the shape of the data
- are clear, but not necessarily neat
- don't require labels or titles (as long as students are clear about what the graphs represent)
- don't require time-consuming attention to color or design

Encourage students to invent different forms of sketch graphs until they discover some that work well in organizing their data. Sketch graphs may be made with pencil and paper, with interlocking cubes, or with stick-on notes. Cubes and stick-on notes in particular offer flexibility because they can easily be rearranged.

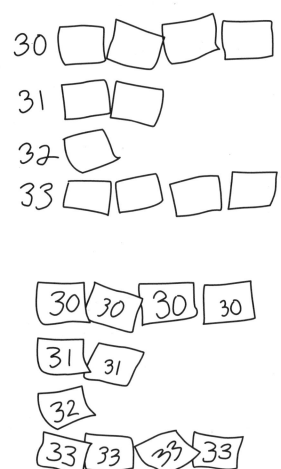

Line Plots: A Quick Way to Show the Shape of the Data

A line plot is a quick way to organize numerical data. It clearly shows the range of the data, the interval from the lowest to the highest value, and how the data are distributed over that range. Line plots work especially well for numerical data with a small range, such as the number of raisins in a box.

A line plot is most often used as a working graph and is especially useful as an initial organizing tool for work with a data set. It need not include a title, labels, or a vertical axis. A line plot is simply a sketch showing the values of the data along a horizontal axis and X's to mark the frequency of those values. For example, a line plot showing the number of raisins in 15 boxes might be drawn as shown below.

From this display, we can quickly see that two-thirds of the boxes have either 37 or 38 raisins.

Although the range is from 30 to 38, the interval in which most data fall is from 35 to 38. The outlier, at 30, appears to be an unusual value, separated by a considerable gap from the rest of the data.

One advantage of a line plot is that each piece of data can be recorded directly on the graph as it is collected. To set up a line plot, students start with an initial guess about what the range of the data is likely to be: What should we put as the lowest number? How high should we go? Leave some room on each end so that you can lengthen the line later if the range includes lower or higher values than you expected.

By quickly sketching data in line plots on the chalkboard, you provide a model of using such graphs to get a quick, clear picture of the shape of the data.

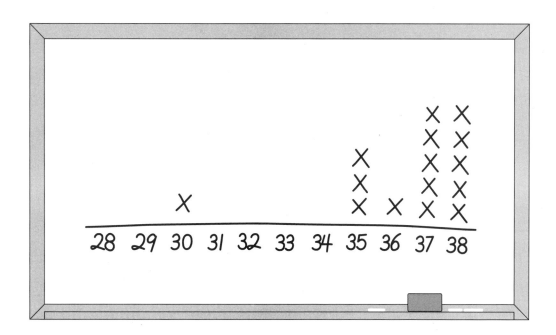

The Shape of the Data: Clumps, Bumps, and Holes

Describing and interpreting data is a skill that must be acquired. Too often, students simply read numbers or other information from a graph or table without any interpretation or understanding. It is easy for students to notice only isolated bits of information ("Vanilla got the most votes" or "Five people were 50 inches tall") without developing an overall sense of what the graph shows. To help students pay attention to the shape of the data—the patterns and special features—we have found useful such words as *clumps, clusters, bumps, gaps, holes, spread out,* and *bunched together.* Encourage students to use this casual language to describe where most of the data are, where there are no data, and where there are isolated pieces of data.

A discussion of the shape of the data often breaks down into two stages. First, we decide what are the special features of the shape: Where are the clumps or clusters, the gaps, the outliers? Are the data spread out, or are lots of the data clustered around a few values? Second, we decide how we can interpret the shape of these data: Do we have theories or experiences that might account for how the data are distributed?

As an example, consider the graph at right, which shows the weight in pounds of 23 lions in U.S. zoos. (Note that this example is for teacher use only; the same data will be presented as Mystery Data in Investigation 2, Landmarks in the Data.) In the first stage of discussion, one group of students observed the following special features:

- There is a clump of lions between 400 and 475 pounds (about a third).
- There is another cluster centering around 300 pounds (another third).
- There are two pairs of much lighter lions, separated by a gap from the rest of the data.

In the second stage of discussion, students considered what might account for the shape of these data. They immediately theorized that the four lightest lions must be cubs. They were, in fact, one litter of 4-month-old cubs in the Miami Zoo. The other two clusters turned out to reflect the difference between the weights of adult male and female lions.

Throughout this unit, we strive to steer students away from merely reading or calculating numbers drawn from their data (the range was 23 to 48, the median was 90, the biggest height was 52 inches). These numbers are useful only when they are seen in the context of the overall shape and patterns of the data and when they lead to questioning and theory building. By focusing instead on the broader picture—the shape of the data—we discover what the data can tell us about the world.

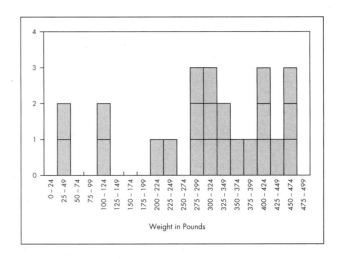

Weight in Pounds

Range and Outliers

Range and *outlier* are two statistical ideas that come up naturally in discussing data with students.

The range of the data is simply the interval from the lowest value to the highest value in the data set. The range of the data in the line plot below, which shows how many raisins were in each of 15 boxes of raisins, is from 30 to 38.

An *outlier* is an individual piece of data that has an unusual value, much lower or much higher than most of the data. It "lies outside" the overall shape and pattern of the data. There is no one definition of how far away from the rest of the data a value must be to be termed an outlier. Although statisticians have rules of thumb for finding outliers, these are always subject to judgment about a particular data set. As you view the shape of the data, you and your stu-

dents must judge whether there are values that don't seem to fit with the rest of the data. For example, in the raisin data, the box containing 30 raisins seems to be an outlier. A family of 12 is likely to be an outlier in family size data.

Both range and outliers are ideas that will come up naturally in this unit. They can be introduced as soon as they arise in the students' descriptions of their data. Students easily learn the correct terms for these ideas and are particularly interested in outliers.

Outliers should be examined closely. Sometimes they turn out to be mistakes—someone counted, measured, or recorded incorrectly—but other times they are simply unusual values. Students are generally very interested in building theories about these odd values: What might account for them?

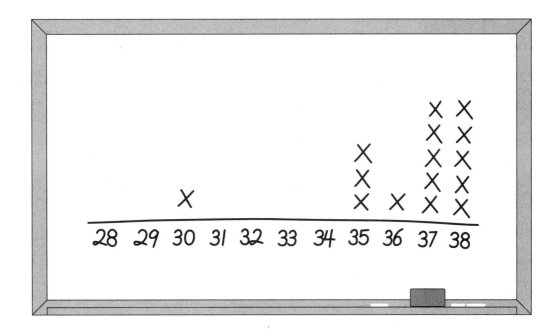

Describing the Shape of the Data

This discussion took place during the activity Describing the Raisin Data (p. 6). Students are looking at their line plot.

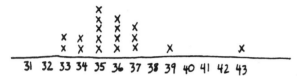

So what can you say about the raisin data? Let's hear a few of your ideas.

Kim: Well, there are a lot at 35.

Alex: There was only one at 39 and one at 43.

Rikki: There are two at 33 and 34.

Karen: And 33 is the lowest.

So no boxes had fewer than 33 raisins?

David: Yeah. And 43 was the highest.

So the range was from 33 to 43. What else?

Jesse: There's nothing at 38, 40, 41, or 42.

Jesse's noticing that there are a lot of holes in this part of the data. Can anyone say any more about that?

Lina Li: Well, there's nothing at 31 or 32 either.

Yes, 33 is the lowest count and there's nothing below it. But the situation that Jesse noticed up here is a little different. What can you say about that?

Kumiko: Mostly, the raisins go from 33 to 37, but sometimes you get something higher.

Can anyone add to that?

B.J.: You'd be really lucky if you were the one who got 43!

Mathematicians have a name for a piece of data that is far away from all the rest. They call it an *outlier.* **An outlier is an unusual piece of data—sometimes it's an error, but sometimes it's just an unusual piece of data. It's often interesting to try to find out more about an outlier. Who had this outlier?**

Emilio: I did. And I counted twice, and Kyle checked it, too, so I know it was 43.

Rikki: Maybe he's got smaller raisins.

Any other theories about Emilio's box?

Lesley Ann: Maybe it doesn't really weigh the same as the other boxes. Maybe too many raisins got dropped in when it was going through the factory.

… [*Later*] So if someone asked you, "What's the typical number of raisins in a box?"—what would you say?

Irena: Well, I'd say 35.

[*Addressing the class as a whole*] **Why would 35 be a reasonable description of how many raisins are in a box?**

DeShane: Because the most boxes had 35.

Any other ways to say this? Or any different ideas?

Kyle: Well, I wouldn't say just 35.

Why not?

Kyle: Well, there's really not that much difference between 33, 34, 35, 36. They're all really close together. I'd say 33 to 37, 'cause the 39 and 43 aren't what you'd usually get.

So Kyle is saying he'd use an interval to describe the raisins, from 33 to 37, and Irena said she'd say 35 was typical. What do other people think about that?

In this discussion, the class has moved gradually from describing individual features of the data to looking at the shape of the data as a whole. The teacher introduced the terms *interval*, *range*, and *outlier* as they came up naturally in the discussion. Throughout, the teacher asked students to give reasons for their ideas and pushed them to think further by asking for additions or alternatives to ideas students raised.

How Many People in a Family?

What Happens

Students decide how to determine family size for their class, then collect family size data in their classroom. They describe the shape of the distribution of family size for their class and determine typical family size from these data. They compare it with the typical family size in their community. Student work focuses on:

- defining the way data will be collected
- making quick sketches of the data
- describing the shape of the data
- summarizing what is typical of the data

 Ten-Minute Math: Estimation and Number Sense Once or twice in the next few days, use this activity. If your class has completed the Fractions unit, *Different Shapes, Equal Pieces*, you may want to do fraction estimation problems.

Present a problem on the chalkboard or overhead, let's say 1/2 + 3/4, and ask:

Is the answer more than one or less than one?

Allow students to think about the problem for about a minute, and then have them discuss it. Encourage students to imagine fraction cards, dot paper squares, or other materials they've used to think about fractions.

Encourage students to give reasons for their answers, such as, "I know it's more than one because 3/4 is bigger than 1/2 and two 1/2's are one."

Ask the same question about other problems, such as

$$1/3 + 1/4 \qquad 2/3 + 2/3 \qquad 7/8 + 1/4 \qquad 4/5 + 5/6$$

Materials

- Unlined paper
- Interlocking cubes (optional)
- Copies of the class list (optional)
- Student Sheet 1 (1 per student, homework)
- Family letter (1 per student)
- Overhead projector
- Blank transparencies and pen

How to Count Who's in Your Family

Begin with a brief discussion of what *typical* means, in the sense of what is most common or usual for a particular group or community. You might talk about a typical lunch or typical clothing for fourth graders in your school, or typical weather in your area at this time of year.

Introduce the data about typical family size that you obtained from your community.

I called City Hall in [name of your town] and asked what the typical family size is in [your town]. They told me the typical family size is about [3]. What do you think they mean by that? How do you think they found out?

After a brief discussion, ask:

Do you think the typical family size for our class might be the same as it is for our town?

Allow students to express their opinions, encouraging them to give reasons.

Let's take a look at the data for our class. If we're going to study family size for this class, how would we count who is in a family?

This question has provoked a lively and extended discussion in every group that has investigated this problem, from third graders to adults. Defining how to count or measure is a critical part of data analysis. Initial decisions about definition profoundly affect the outcomes of many statistical studies. Allow 15–20 minutes for discussion and 5–10 minutes for coming to a decision about how to count family members.

Help the students arrive at a consensus about a definition of family size. Try to avoid voting as a means of settling disagreements; help students to determine instead what aspects of family size they are most interested in. The object is not to arrive at the same definition the U.S. Census Bureau uses, but to arrive at a definition that the class as a whole decides is reasonable for their purposes. See the **Teacher Note,** Who Is in Your Family? (p. 18) for a discussion of possible definitions.

Counting People in Your Family Using the consensus definition, students record their names and family size in a display where everyone can see it. (Students can copy the data on a class list for the small-group work.)

If you have interlocking or other cubes, each student might build a tower to represent his or her family, one cube per family member. Then the towers can be arranged in a sequence or in groups to show how many families of each size there are.

Students work in small groups to represent and describe the class data. Each group makes a sketch or picture of the data in at least two ways. Encourage students to use the line plot, demonstrated in the raisins investigation. A concrete material, such as interlocking cubes, provides another excellent way of displaying family size. This is a good opportunity for students to invent new ways to display their data. Each group writes a description of the data, based on their representations, and makes a joint decision about how best to describe the typical family size for the class.

What's the Shape of These Data?

Interpreting the Data After students have finished their displays and descriptions, ask for reports from the small groups.

What did you notice about our data? What did you choose for a typical family size? Why?

Ask students to give reasons for their decisions, and encourage them to ask questions of each other about their choices. In this discussion, students often express informally some important ideas about how to summarize data, such as looking at the middle of the data, or at where the data are "clumped." Some examples of student responses are as follows:

> The smallest family is two and the largest is ten, so I picked six because it's right in the middle between two and ten.
>
> Most families in our class have four people, so I think four is the most usual family size.
>
> There are a lot at three and a lot at four, so I'd say three and a half.

For an idea of what is important in this discussion, see the **Teacher Note,** Summarizing Data: What's Typical? (p. 19).

How does the typical family size in this class compare to the statistic about typical family size in our community? Are they different or similar? Why might this be true?

Guide the discussion with additional questions as needed, for example:

What kinds of people live in the community who aren't represented in our class or even in our school? [people without children, people with grown children] Do you think the family size in our class is like the family size of other classes in the school?

How Many Brothers and Sisters?

We're going to collect some additional data about our families for our homework assignment. How many brothers and sisters do you have? Do you think there will be more or fewer brothers and sisters than there were people in our families? Why?

Students may want to discuss how to define brothers and sisters, just as they did for families. Allow some discussion, but encourage the class to agree on a definition for the homework assignment.

Have each student report how many brothers and sisters he or she has. (Some students may need to be reminded not to count themselves.) Record the numbers on the board or on the overhead projector, and have the students copy them for their homework assignment. If you want students to copy them on a class list, ask them to report their information in the class list order.

Sessions 2 and 3 Follow-Up

 **Homework**

How Many Brothers and Sisters?   Student Sheet 1, How Many Brothers and Sisters?, gives students further practice with organizing and making sense of data, as they make a line plot of class data about brothers and sisters. They also write brief statements about the typical number of siblings for their class. Along with the student sheet, students should take home the data sheet they made in class. They should also take home the family letter or *Investigations* at Home.

❖ **Tip for the Linguistically Diverse Classroom** Allow students to use their native languages in writing what is typical for their class, supplementing their work with a visual indication of the "typical" number on their line plot.

Students may want to ask their parents or other adults how many brothers and sisters they have and compare those numbers to the class numbers. (Adult data could be added to the class line plot in a different color.)

The next session begins with a discussion of the homework.

Extensions

Adding More Family Data   Many classes have become interested in surveying other classes in the school, comparing the data, and compiling the data from many classes to see what the typical family size is for a larger number of students.

Census Data   Students might also enjoy a study of the census. Your city or town can provide you with local information from the most recent census. For national data, contact Customer Services, U.S. Bureau of Census, Washington, D.C. 20233. Your students may be interested in a few items of census data other than family size.

Students are usually eager to discuss their families. As this is a topic of intense personal interest and concern, allow adequate time for everyone to participate in the discussion. Diversity in family structure is to be expected and respected. Students may bring up many kinds of family situations. What about grandparents, aunts, or uncles who live with them? If we're going to count Nick's grandmother who lives with him, what about Irena's grandfather who lives upstairs from her, or Rafael's aunt with whom he spends the summers? Students often talk about parts of their families living in different locations ("When I'm at my dad's house, there are three of us there, but when I'm at my mom's, there are four of us"). Older siblings who no longer live at home, foster children, people temporarily living with the family, permanent members of the household who are not relatives, and even pets have been brought up in these discussions.

Teachers can handle these discussions sensitively so that all family styles and arrangements are acknowledged and accepted. But eventually students must come to some consensus about a definition of family. There is, of course, no single right way to construct this definition. Choices some classes have made include: "You and your parents and your sisters and brothers, regardless of where they live"; "Everyone who lives in your house right now"; or, as one group of adults finally decided, "Everyone who uses the same bathroom as you"! The definition can be constructed to reflect what the students are most interested in. Discourage students from voting on a definition. As amateur statisticians, students should select a definition not because it is the most popular, but because it will help them collect data that will give them the information they want.

Summarizing Data: What's Typical?

Summarizing data is one of the main tasks of data analysis. A data set starts out as an unordered set of many values; we need to capture the essence of the shape of the data through a few key numbers so that we can describe and compare data sets without referring to all the values.

As consumers of statistics, our encounters with data sets are often through these key numbers: The average (mean) number of people in a U.S. household in 1990 was 2.61; in the same year, the median income of U.S. families was $35,353; also in 1990, more women in the U.S. work force were employed in "administrative support" than in any other category of occupation, while the mode for men was the category of "precision production, craft, and repair" (source of data: U.S. Department of Commerce, Bureau of the Census).

Statisticians try to capture the essence of the data by identifying its center, or average, and then describing how the data are spread around that center. We are used to thinking of average as the arithmetic mean, the number obtained by adding all the values and dividing by the number of values. Actually, there are many possible measures of average, including the mean, median, and mode. The median, which students will learn about in Investigation 2, is the middle of the data when all the data are put in order. The mode is the most frequently occurring value and is used most often with non-numerical data, such as eye color, birth month, or career choice.

Deciding what is usual, typical, or central for a group is one reason to summarize data. Students will encounter the question "What's typical?" in many of their data analysis investigations. To compare two sets of data, they will also find it necessary to summarize each data set. For example, to determine whether the number of people per household in the U.S. is increasing or decreasing, we must summarize and compare data sets from different years.

Students begin to understand how to summarize data by developing their own approaches during the investigations. For example, when comparing the heights of first and fourth graders, one fourth grader hit upon an important notion about how to summarize a data set: "We should find the number that's maybe in the middle or that all the other numbers are crowded around."

In Investigation 2, Landmarks in the Data, students will work with the median, a powerful and developmentally appropriate average for use at the upper elementary grades. Understanding the median builds on the informal ideas about the center of the data that students develop in the first investigation.

Some of your students may already know how to compute the arithmetic mean (they may know it as the average). Although this type of average is often taught in elementary school, research has shown that the nature and significance of the mean is often not understood, even by older students and adults.

We recommend that teachers discourage any use of the mean until students have had a lot of exposure to data analysis. Students need experience with a great variety of data sets before they are ready to understand how the arithmetic mean relates to the data it represents. Discourage students from applying the add-'em-all-up-and-divide-by-the-number-of-values approach. If a student says, "We could find the average," you can respond something like this: "Yes, we could. Actually, there are many kinds of averages that you'll learn about as you go on in mathematics. Averages are ways of saying what's typical about a set of data. Right now we're going to be inventing our own ways of deciding what's typical, and later in this unit you're going to learn about one kind of average."

INVESTIGATION 2

Landmarks in the Data

What Happens

Session 1: How Tall Are Fourth Graders?
Students measure their own heights. They record their heights on a line plot, in a table, or with tallies. They describe the data and summarize what's typical of them. They discuss methods for solving the problem: How much taller is a fourth grader than a first grader?

Sessions 2 and 3: Fourth and First Graders: How Much Taller? Students collect height data from a first grade class or classes. They organize the data with a quick sketch, identifying clumps, bumps, holes, the range of the data, and any outliers. Students compare the data set for the first graders with that for the fourth graders. They prepare and present reports illustrating their methods of comparing the two data sets.

Session 4: Looking at Mystery Data Students examine three sets of Mystery Data, each giving the length or height of individuals in some group of living things. Students describe the data and construct a theory about what the living things are. A fourth set of Mystery Data can be used for further group work or individual homework.

Session 5: Finding the Median Students are introduced to the median as a formal measure that statisticians use to summarize a set of data. They find the median height for the class. They find the median height of the '93 NBA All-Stars and compare it to the median height of the class. They find the medians for the data they collected in earlier investigations.

Sessions 6 and 7: Using Landmarks in Data Students examine another set of mystery data, describe the landmarks, and establish what the data represent. They use the median to compare the weights of cats and lions. They investigate the question: Who has more cavities, the Massachusetts group (Student Sheet 11) or our class?

Mathematical Emphasis

- Describing the shape of the data
- Summarizing to express what is typical of the data
- Inventing ways to compare two sets of data by describing the shape of the data and what's typical of the data
- Using linear measurement
- Inventing representations to compare two sets of data
- Representing data through sketches
- Revising and refining sketches to make a presentation graph or chart
- Visualizing and estimating lengths and heights
- Using the median to describe a set of data and to compare one data set to another
- Understanding that the median is only one landmark in the data
- Finding the median in a set of data arranged in numerical order (e.g., when students line up in order by height)
- Finding the median in a set of data grouped by frequency (e.g., on a line plot or other graph)

What to Plan Ahead of Time

Materials

- Chart paper for recording data (Session 1, optional)
- Unlined paper for sketching the data (Sessions 1–7)
- Measuring tools—tape measures, yardsticks, or metersticks—for each small group of students (Sessions 1–4)
- Calculators (Sessions 6–7)
- Colored markers or crayons and graph paper for making presentation graphs (Sessions 2–3)
- Overhead projector (Session 4)
- Interlocking cubes, counting chips, or other concrete materials for making models of the data (Session 5)
- Class data saved from Investigation 1: empty raisin boxes, family-size data, and data on brothers and sisters (Sessions 1, 5)

Other Preparation

- Make copies of your class list for recording data, 1 per student. (Session 1, optional)
- Make copies of the first grade class list, 1 per student. (Sessions 2–3, optional)
- Arrange with the first grade teacher(s) a way for your students to collect the heights of first graders. (Sessions 2–3)
- Before Session 4, become familiar with the Mystery Data sets on Student Sheets 4–7.
- Before Sessions 6–7, be sure students know how many cavities they have had.

- Duplicate student sheets and teaching resources (located at the end of this unit) as follows. If you have Student Activity Booklets, copy only the items marked with an asterisk.

For Session 1

Student Sheet 2, Heights of Two Fourth Grade Classes (p. 74): 1 per student

Student Sheet 3, How Tall Are Fourth Graders? (p. 75): 1 per student (homework)

For Sessions 2–3

One-centimeter graph paper (p. 91): 3–4 per student (for throughout the investigation)

For Session 4

Student Sheet 4, Mystery Data A (p. 76): 1 per student, and 1 transparency*

Student Sheet 5, Mystery Data B (p. 77): 1 per student, and 1 transparency*

Student Sheet 6, Mystery Data C (p. 78): 1 per student, and 1 transparency*

Student Sheet 7, Looking at Mystery Data (p. 79): 1 per student (homework)

For Sessions 5

Student Sheet 8, How Many Cavities? (p. 80): 1 per student (homework)

'93 All-Star Cards* (pp. 84–86): 1 set. Cut apart ahead of time.

For Sessions 6–7

Student Sheet 9, Cat Weights (p. 81): 1 per student

Student Sheet 10, Another Mystery (p. 82): 1 per student

Student Sheet 11, Cavity Data (p. 83): 1 per student

How Tall Are Fourth Graders?

Materials

- Completed homework from Investigation 1
- Measuring tools
- Unlined paper
- Student Sheet 2 (1 per student)
- Student Sheet 3 (1 per student, homework)
- Chart paper (optional)
- Copies of the class list (optional)

What Happens

Students measure their own heights. They record their heights on a line plot, in a table, or with tallies. They describe the data and summarize what's typical of them. They discuss methods for solving the problem: How much taller is a fourth grader than a first grader? Student work focuses on:

- measuring accurately
- recording and describing data
- identifying what's typical of a data set
- proposing methods to solve a problem

 Ten-Minute Math: Estimation and Number Sense   During the next few days, continue to practice this activity with fractions. Remember to find time for it outside the math hour.

Present a problem on the chalkboard or overhead, let's say ½ + ¼, and ask:

Is the answer closer to 0, 1, or 2?

Give students about a minute to think about the problem and then have them discuss what they know. Encourage students to imagine fraction strips or other materials they've used to think about fractions.

Encourage students to give reasons for their answers; for example, "I know it's closer to 1 because ¼ is less than ½ and when they're added together, it will be close to 1, but not quite."

Ask the same question about other problems. For example:

$$\frac{1}{8} + \frac{1}{8} \qquad \frac{3}{4} + \frac{1}{8} \qquad \frac{7}{8} + \frac{1}{24} \qquad \frac{9}{10} + \frac{14}{15}$$

Ask students to take out their homework from yesterday about the brothers and sisters data. Ask them to share how they organized the data and made the line plots.

Have several students read their sentences describing what is typical for the class. Discuss any differences in conclusions, asking students to give reasons for their conclusions.

Ask students to look at the shape of the data in their line plots. Do they notice any clumps, bumps, or holes? How did looking at the shape of the data help them make their statements about what's typical?

If students collected additional data from adults, have them explain how they recorded those data on their line plot. How do these data compare to the class data?

Collect the homework and review it. Do students seem to understand how to make a line plot? Do they see some need to put the numbers in order? Are the plots fairly neat and easy to read with X's (or other tally marks) fairly well aligned? What kinds of statements have the students made about what's typical? Are they reasonable? Do the students seem to be observing the shape of the data or looking at individual pieces of data?

Sometimes we collect data in order to compare one group with another. For example, we could use your raisin data and compare them with a different brand of raisins, or we could compare your family data with data for a younger or older group of students, or with students who live somewhere else.

Today we're going to start working on a problem that involves comparing two sets of data: How much taller is a fourth grader than a first grader? First we'll collect some initial data—your heights; then we'll plan how to do the rest of the investigation.

Have a couple of pairs of students demonstrate measuring each other's height, asking students to discuss the methods they will use. Will shoes be on or off? What units of measurement will they use? Will they measure to the closest inch, half inch, quarter inch? Resist the temptation to raise questions yourself; support students as they raise and resolve their own questions.

Comparing Metersticks and Yardsticks Distribute tape measures, metersticks, or yardsticks. If you have separate metersticks and yardsticks, ask students to compare the two tools. If you have combination tools (inches on one side, centimeters on the other), ask students to look at both sides and talk about the differences. If no one comments on the tape you have used to cover the end of the yardstick side, call attention to it.

Why do you think I covered the end, from 36 inches on?

Explain that when we are measuring in inches and feet, 36 is an important landmark number because it is equal to 3 feet. You might add that these sticks are actually metersticks (100 centimeters long), and 1 meter is more than 36 inches, so you covered the end to make 36 be the end point on the yardstick side.

If students are using such combination tools to measure each other's height in feet and inches, they will need to remember to line up the second yardstick from the 36—not from the very end of the stick. You may want to demonstrate how to measure something taller than 36 inches with this sort of tool.

Collecting Initial Data Students work in groups of three to measure their own heights. One student is measured, one student does the measuring, and the third checks the accuracy of the measurement and records it. You can greatly facilitate the measuring process by tacking to a wall large pieces of paper on which students can mark their heights. See the **Teacher Note,** Measuring Heights: Using Tools (p. 26), for a discussion of some confusions that may arise when students have tools with two different scales.

Observe students as they measure each other. Discuss any problems that arise during the process.

Note: In this investigation, it is assumed that most students will measure their heights in inches rather than centimeters. There are a couple of reasons we have chosen U.S. Standard measures rather than metric: In the United States, heights are still commonly measured in inches; and all the other data we will be using in the investigation are reported in U.S. Standard units. You may prefer to have students measure in centimeters. If so, you will have to either skip the activity, Comparing Our Class with Other Fourth Grades, at the end of this session, or convert the data on Student Sheet 2 to centimeters. (Please do not ask your students to do the conversion.)

Describing the Class Height Data

Ask students to report the results of measuring each other. Have the students record all the data for themselves as you record it on the chalkboard (they will need the data for homework). Students may record the data on a class list so they have each individual's height, or they may record the data without names. (Consider whether some students would be sensitive to having their heights recorded by their names.) If you record the data on a class list, have heights reported in that order.

Ask students how you might organize and represent the data so everyone can see it. Students might suggest a line plot, a table, or tallies. Choose one of their suggestions to record the class data.

What can you say about how tall people in our class are?

Encourage students to describe the overall shape of the data—the range, how it clumps or spreads out, whether there are any outliers—and to summarize what's typical of the data as a group. Ask for reasons supporting their choices for typical values. See the **Dialogue Box**, Discussing Invented Methods for Finding Typical Values (p. 27). In discussing outliers, watch for sensitive situations; be sure to refer to data points, not individuals, as outliers, and have students do the same.

Comparing Our Class with Other Fourth Grades

Give out copies of Student Sheet 2, Heights of Two Fourth Grade Classes. In small groups, students compare their own data with these fourth grade data. How would they describe the differences and similarities? Have students share their comments with the whole class.

❖ **Tip for the Linguistically Diverse Classroom** In small group discussions like this, encourage students who are proficient in English to help nonnative speakers communicate their ideas nonverbally—for example, by pointing to elements of the line plots—and to help them verbalize what they are seeing.

Session 1 Follow-Up

How Tall Are Fourth Graders? Student Sheet 3, How Tall Are Fourth Graders?, asks students to make a quick sketch of the height data from their own class. Encourage them to do it in a different way than was done in class. Remember to send home the class height data, along with the student sheet.

 **Homework**

During this investigation, you will probably discover that many students have difficulty with linear measurement. Teachers commonly find that some of their upper elementary students:

- combine metric and U.S. Standard systems ("I'm 48 inches and 1 centimeter tall.")

- do not distinguish between metric and U.S. Standard units ("I'm 125 inches tall.")

- do not know how to combine two parts of the measurement ("I'm 6 inches taller than one yardstick—how do I do that?")

- measure from the wrong end of the ruler or yardstick (as Sarah and Nick explain in the sample dialogue below)

Don't be alarmed! Such difficulties are common among students who have had little experience with measuring. Use this investigation as an opportunity for students to gain experience and to help one another be accurate. Observe their work and listen to their comments and questions. Ask them to discuss and check accuracy as they work in small groups. Have students share the difficulties they encounter. Support those who use their own experience and knowledge to check the reasonableness of their measurements, as in this sample discussion:

Anyone else come up with a problem they had to solve when they were measuring?

Sarah: Yeah, we did. We measured me and we came out to 57 inches, and I know I'm not 57 inches.

How do you know?

Sarah: Because my mom keeps a chart of all the kids and we mark it on our birthdays, and I know I'm shorter than that. On my birthday I was 51.

Nick: And also Sarah's one of the shortest in our class, and 57 wouldn't be near to the shortest height in the class.

So you realized that 57 inches wasn't reasonable? Did you figure out what happened?

Sarah: Yeah. When we measured the first part and then we moved the ruler up to measure the rest, we flipped it around and we had the ruler going in the wrong direction.

Oh, you mean you measured from the end of the yardstick that says 36?

Nick: Yeah, we got to 36 and then we swung it around like this, so we were measuring from 36 up, and we marked the second part at 21, so we had 36 plus 21 inches and we got 57. But we were going the wrong way.

For many teachers, it helps to think of students' initial measurements as first approximations of their answers, rather than final results. A vital part of their learning is the opportunity to discuss the reasonableness of their measurements, to measure several times, and to correct their mistakes. When students feel the results matter, they become much more precise.

A teacher's role in this process is delicate. Your students will need to discuss their methods (Should they use the yardstick? The foot ruler? Should they stand against the wall?) as well as their results. Ask questions that focus on whether their results make sense (Is Marci about the same height as Shiro? Is Vanessa that much taller than Qi Sun?).

DIALOGUE BOX

Discussing Invented Methods for Finding Typical Values

During the activity Describing the Class Height Data (p. 25), these students are talking about the shape of their data as sketched on a line plot. They are trying to find a "typical" height for their class.

Ahmad: We think you should pick a number that comes up the most, so we picked 52, because there are more 52's than any other number.

What does everyone else think about that method?

Pinsuba: We did the same thing. There are a lot of 52's, so that seemed like what was typical.

Did anybody make a different choice?

Karen: We came out with 58.

So your choice is a little higher than what Ahmad's group picked. Why do you think that's reasonable?

Karen: I don't know. It just seemed like that would be it.

But I'm interested in your reason for 58. [*Pause. Still no response from the student.*] I see a big clump of data between 56 and 59.

Karen: Yeah, the clump seems like it's crowded around 58.

Yes, that's an interesting method. I can see your reasons for both of these methods. Does anyone have a good argument for choosing one over the other for the most typical value for our class?

Jesse: Well, even though 52 has the most, there are still only six kids at 52, but there are 12 kids bunched around 58.

So you'd choose the biggest clump of data?

[Later in the same discussion]

Qi Sun: Our group chose 62.

What were your reasons?

Qi Sun: A lot of kids got 62, and also it's the highest number.

You chose the highest number?

Qi Sun: Yes, because a bunch of kids got it.

What do some of you who picked numbers in the 50's think about that?

Rafael: I don't think you should pick the highest, because that's not what's typical. Most kids aren't that tall.

Marci: Yeah, like with the families, the typical size wasn't the smallest or the largest, but somewhere in the middle.

So you think a middle value is more typical. What do you think about that argument, Qi Sun?

Qi Sun: Yeah, maybe.

So you noticed that four kids were 62 inches tall; that's an important part of the shape of these data. But Marci and Rafael are arguing that with these data, a typical value wouldn't be that high.

This discussion can be difficult for the teacher because, while there is certainly no single right answer, students may come up with unreasonable approaches. Encourage all invented methods; many of the students' ideas will help them understand standard measures of center such as the median, which they will encounter in Session 5 of this investigation, and the mode, which they will encounter in a later unit.

However, do not let students get the message that any method is as good as any other; expect them to reflect on whether or not their results are reasonable and useful. Juxtaposing one student method with another, as the teacher does in this discussion, is often a good way to help students think about the reasonableness of their method.

Fourth and First Graders: How Much Taller?

Materials

- Measuring tools
- Unlined paper
- Graph paper
- Colored markers or crayons
- First grade class list (optional)
- Sketch of height data from their class (Session 1 homework)

What Happens

Students collect height data from a first grade class or classes. They organize it with a quick sketch, identifying clumps, bumps, holes, the range of the data, and any outliers. The students compare the data set for the first graders with that for the fourth graders. They prepare and present reports illustrating their methods of comparing the two data sets. Student work focuses on:

- measuring accurately
- comparing two sets of data
- preparing presentation graphs and reports

How would we figure out how much taller fourth graders are than first graders?

Encourage students to suggest methods for solving this problem. See the **Dialogue Box,** How Can We Compare Our Class with a First Grade Class? (p. 32).

As students think about the problem, they may question the accuracy of their own height data. Some students may suggest remeasuring everyone. Or some may feel they need more data from students in their own grade. If possible, support any decisions along these lines.

Doing the Measurement Decide with the students and the first grade teacher(s) how to collect the first grade height data. The first graders could come for a visit to your classroom, or teams of students could visit them. *It is very important that all students participate in some way in measuring first graders so that they have a feel for the data.*

Have the data recorded in a central location or on a class list that can be duplicated for each small group.

Measuring First Graders' Heights

Working with the data from their Session 1 homework and the data they collected in the preceding activity, students do the following in their small groups:

- Examine sketches of the data for their own heights that they made for homework.
- Make quick sketches of the data for first grade heights. This might be done in several ways.
- Analyze the shape of each data set. Where are the clumps, bumps, holes? What is the range? Are there any outliers?
- Decide on a method to compare the two data sets.
- Try out the chosen method. See if the result is reasonable. Try a different method, if needed.

Circulate while students work in their small groups. Emphasize the importance of coming up with a good method for solving the problem, not just an answer. Remind students of methods they have used to identify a typical value in other data that might work here as well.

Comparing Two Sets of Data

Publishing Findings

When each group of students has worked with the data long enough to settle on a way of comparing the two data sets, they can decide how to represent and report their findings.

Each small group makes a presentation graph or chart to show the data and to illustrate their method for comparing the two sets. Encourage students to experiment with different ways to present their data, making at least one rough draft before starting a final presentation graph. A group may find more than one good way of showing the data. Encourage inventiveness and clarity. Each group also writes a description of their method to go with their representation of the data. See the **Teacher Note**, Presentation Graphs: Inventiveness and Clarity (p. 31).

You may have each group present their findings to the rest of the class. Often, however, such presentations are much less interesting than the discussion and interaction that went on within the groups. Posting the representations and explanations on the bulletin board and giving students time to examine them may be sufficient. As an alternative, hold a brief evaluation conference with each group, just as you might do to evaluate a piece of writing.

Presentation Graphs: Inventiveness and Clarity

Like the final draft of an essay, a presentation graph is meant to be received by an audience. Its purpose is to present an organized, clear, and accessible display of the data. It supports what students have found in their analysis by directing attention to important features of the data.

Constructing presentation graphs to show how data compare is an opportunity for inventiveness and creativity. The task seems to inspire students and teachers alike.

Below is a graph that fourth grade students made to show the comparison of first graders' and fourth graders' heights. Their variation on a standard bar graph format provides a clear picture of the distribution of the two groups' heights, showing where the two data sets do and do not overlap.

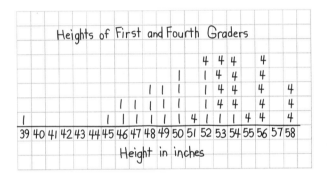

Another group invented this vertical graph (at right), also quite effective, to show the comparison between data sets. What is powerful about both of these graphs is that they clearly present the important information about the data.

Color can be a wonderful tool for revealing features of the data. In the first height graph shown here, students could have used two different colors rather than writing 1's and 4's to differentiate the two data sets. However, some students become bogged down in coloring or decorating graphs in ways that obscure rather than illuminate the data. Encourage students to design their graphs carefully to highlight important features of the data.

If a computer is available, graphing software provides one option for students as they create their presentation graphs. Some students may enjoy and benefit from the clarity, neatness, and precision that graphing software provides. However, the software appropriate for the elementary grades limits students to straightforward representations of standard tables and graphs, such as bar graphs.

The invented graphs shown here could not have been made with graphing software. If you use a computer, encourage a mixture of student-generated and computer-generated graphs, and help students see the limitations as well as the advantages of graphs made on the computer.

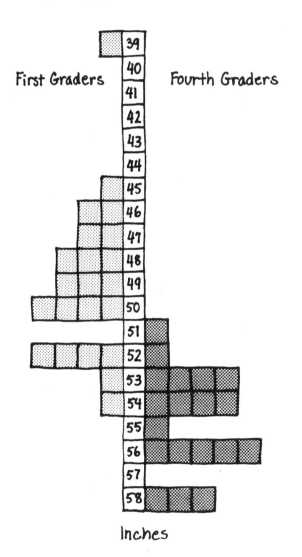

How Can We Compare Our Class with a First Grade Class?

This discussion took place in Session 2, during the activity Comparing Two Sets of Data (p. 29).

So what kinds of plans can we make for figuring out how much taller our class is than Ms. Rivera's first graders?

Rashaida: We should measure all the first graders and all of us.

Luisa: We could pair everyone up.

Pair everyone? How would that work?

Luisa: Like the shortest with the shortest and the tallest with the tallest.

Oh, so you'd put everyone in order by height and pair up the shortest first grader with the shortest fourth grader? Then what?

Luisa: You could subtract.

Luisa's suggesting we pair up first graders and fourth graders in order. [Writes on the board: Pair up first graders and fourth graders.] Does anyone have some other ideas about that?

Joey: Well, it's not exactly like that. But my idea is that you'd find the medium ones, like there's the shortest and there's the tallest, but that's not what's really typical, so you look at the mediums.

You'd compare the medium first graders and the medium fourth graders? [Writes on board: Compare medium first and fourth graders.] Other ideas?

Rikki: We could find the one number that's sort of in the middle or that the other numbers are crowded around, and then do the same thing for the first grade and then subtract.

Can you say a little more about that?

Rikki: You'd get all the heights and you'd put them on a graph, all in order, and then you'd look for maybe the middle number or a big clump where most of the heights are.

OK. I'm not sure if that's one idea or two different ideas. [Writes: Use middle height; Look for a clump where most heights are.] Who else has a plan for comparing this class and the first graders?

At this point, the teacher is not pushing for complete, detailed plans, but is trying to get out a variety of basic approaches. Students will work in small groups to develop a more detailed plan later. The list from this brainstorming session will provide starting points for the small-group work.

Ways to Compare
- Pair up first graders and fourth graders
- Compare medium first and fourth graders
- Use middle height
- Look for a clump where most heights are

Looking at Mystery Data

What Happens

Students examine three sets of Mystery Data, each giving the length or height of individuals in some group of living things. Students describe the data and construct a theory about what the living things are. A fourth set of Mystery Data can be used for individual homework. Student work focuses on:

- describing the shape of the data
- summarizing what is typical of the data
- examining the relationship between grouped and ungrouped data
- visualizing and estimating lengths and heights

 Ten-Minute Math: Broken Calculator   Once or twice during the next few days, at a time other than the math hour, do Broken Calculator problems.

Pose the problem.

I want to make 56 using my calculator, but the 5 and 6 keys are broken. How can I use my calculator to do this?

Students solve the problem by themselves.

Record their solutions on the board. Examples might be as follows:

$49 + 7$ $70 - 14$ $2 \times 30 - 4$ $112 \div 2$ 8×7

If there is time, students choose one of these approaches and try to find a series of solutions that are related so they follow a pattern (the broken calculator is now fixed so you can use the 5 and 6 keys). Not all the solutions lead easily to a pattern, and some patterns end after only a few examples.

$49 + 7$	$70 - 14$	$2 \times 30 - 4$
$48 + 8$	$71 - 15$	$3 \times 20 - 4$
$47 + 9$	$72 - 16$	$4 \times 15 - 4$
$46 + 10$	$73 - 17$	$5 \times 12 - 4$

Materials

- Student Sheet 4 (1 per student)
- Student Sheet 5 (1 per student)
- Student Sheet 6 (1 per student)
- Student Sheet 7 (1 per student, homework)
- Transparencies for Student Sheets 4–6
- Overhead projector
- Measuring tools
- Unlined paper

Describing Mystery Data A

Hand out copies of Student Sheet 4, Mystery Data A, and show it on the overhead projector during the discussion.

Note: Each set of Mystery Data is presented in two ways—a table of individual values (ungrouped data), and a line plot showing how often each value occurs (grouped data). Both representations are commonly used to convey information; students should be aware of the differences between them.

This page shows the measurements of 24 individual members of some group of living things. Your task is to develop a theory about what this group might be by looking carefully at the data.

In the table, each row shows the measurement of some thing that was measured. The line plot shows the same data in a different way. Don't tell me any of your theories yet about what these things might be. First, what can you say about these data? How would you describe them?

Encourage students to use what they know about their own heights to estimate and visualize how tall or long the mystery beings might be. See the **Dialogue Box,** Visualizing Measurement Data (p. 38).

Now that we have a good sense of how tall or long these mystery beings are, let's brainstorm about what they could be. I'm interested in your theories, but I'm also interested in your reasons for your theories and whether you agree or disagree with theories other people come up with.

Record students' theories in a place where they can remain posted. Keep the identity of this first set a mystery for now.

Teacher Checkpoint

Mystery Data B and C

Hand out Student Sheets 5 and 6, Mystery Data B and C, and show them in turn on the overhead projector. Make measurement tools available.

These Mystery Data sets represent two more groups of living things. Your job is to describe the data carefully and then figure out what these things could possibly be. Maybe no one will discover the right answer— and that's OK. Your theory can be either strange or ordinary, as long as you can make a good argument that your theory fits the data.

Working in small groups, students describe each data set and develop theories about what living things the data could represent.

Listen to the students' theories. Are they proposing ideas that are genuine possibilities? Are they using information they already know about the heights of other living objects? Are they supporting their guesses with plausible reasons?

Data Stories   For each of the three sets of Mystery Data, students write "the story of the data," including a description of the data, how the measurements compare to others they know about (for example, their own heights), their theories about what the data might represent, and reasons for their theories. You might make a display showing the data and student stories.

❖   **Tip for the Linguistically Diverse Classroom**   Students who have limited proficiency in English might contribute to the small-group discussion by sketching their ideas about what the Mystery Data represent. For writing the story of the data, pair students who have limited English proficiency with those who write comfortably in English. Their story can be presented as a combination of words and simple drawings.

The Mysteries Revealed   Emphasize that there was no way to know for sure what these Mystery Data represent. The task was to develop theories that really matched the data.

Now we're going to try to get closer to what these things really are. To narrow down the possibilities, I'm going to give you some clues.

Discuss one data set at a time. Using the clues, students can eliminate some of the theories they have developed and feel more sure about others. You may want to devise your own clues if you wish.

- Mystery Data A: They were all in Salt Lake City at the same time on February 21, 1993.
- Mystery Data B: They are not human. They live in zoos and museums in the United States.
- Mystery Data C: These data were collected in 1989. If we measured these same living things now, the data would be different.

See the **Teacher Note,** About the Mystery Data (p. 36), to get further ideas for clues. You could play a game of Twenty Questions to reveal the mysteries for each data set, or you could give more clues until the students uncover the mystery. You may want to reveal the solution dramatically, placing the answer in a sealed envelope that a student can open and read to the class.

❖   **Tip for the Linguistically Diverse Classroom**   When presenting clues, make use of pointing, modeling, and visual aids such as maps and pictures. When you finally reveal the answers, show pictures of a basketball player, a boa constrictor, a newborn, and a tree.

Session 4 Follow-Up

 **Homework**

Looking at Mystery Data Student Sheet 7, Looking at Mystery Data, asks students to construct a theory about another set of height data. Students study and then describe the data as they do in the classroom activities for Mystery Data A, B, and C. If you want to use the completed homework sheet in a follow-up classroom activity, you can refer to the appropriate notes in the **Teacher Note** below, About the Mystery Data.

Teacher Note ⟩ ***About the Mystery Data***

To the teacher: STOP! Don't look!

Before you read the following descriptions of the Mystery Data sets (Student Sheets 4–7) and ruin the surprise, don't you want to try solving the mysteries yourself?

The Mystery Data sheets each contain measurements of individuals in some real group of living things. The living things in each set are closely related in some way. Each group is something about which data may logically be collected—not some random assortment of disparate things, such as a bear, a camel, a moose, and a zebra. The students' job is to develop a theory about what each set of Mystery Data might represent.

The first three data sets are displayed in two ways: (1) a table of the data, in which each row shows a single value, and (2) a line plot of the data, with the values grouped to show the frequency with which each value occurs in the data set. Mystery Data sets A, B, and C are to be used for small-group work in Session 4. Looking at Mystery Data is a set that you may want to use for homework at the end of the investigation.

Mystery Data A (Student Sheet 4)

These values are the heights of the 24 basketball players who were selected to play in the 1993 NBA All-Star Game on February 21, 1993, in Salt Lake City, Utah. The West team won, 135–132.

West Team	Height	Position, Team
Charles Barkley	78" (6'6")	forward, Phoenix Suns
Clyde Drexler	79" (6'7")	guard, Portland Trail Blazers
Sean Elliott	80" (6'8")	forward, San Antonio Spurs
Tim Hardaway	72" (6'0")	guard, Golden State Warriors
Shawn Kemp	82" (6'10")	forward, Seattle SuperSonics
Dan Majerle	78" (6'6")	guard, Phoenix Suns
Karl Malone	81" (6'9")	forward, Utah Jazz
Danny Manning	82" (6'10")	forward, Los Angeles Clippers
Hakeem Olajuwon	84" (7'0")	center, Houston Rockets
Terry Porter	75" (6'3")	guard, Portland Trail Blazers
David Robinson	85" (7'1")	center, San Antonio Spurs
John Stockton	73" (6'1")	guard, Utah Jazz

East Team	Height	Position, Team
Brad Dougherty	84" (7'0")	center, Cleveland Cavaliers
Joe Dumars	75" (6'3")	guard, Detroit Pistons
Patrick Ewing	84" (7'0")	center, New York Knicks
Larry Johnson	79" (6'7")	forward, Charlotte Hornets
Michael Jordan	78" (6'6")	guard, Chicago Bulls
Larry Nance	82" (6'10")	forward, Cleveland Cavaliers
Shaquille O'Neal	85" (7'1")	center, Orlando Magic
Scottie Pippen	79" (6'7")	forward, Chicago Bulls
Mark Price	72" (6'0")	guard, Cleveland Cavaliers
Isiah Thomas	73" (6'1")	guard, Detroit Pistons
Detlef Schrempf	82" (6'10")	forward, Indiana Pacers
Dominique Wilkins	80" (6'8")	forward, Atlanta Hawks

[Source: *Boston Herald* sports department.]

Continued on next page

Mystery Data B (Student Sheet 5)

These values are the lengths of 18 boa constrictors living in various museums or zoos in the United States.

Name	Length	Location
Shannon	116" (9'8")	Boston Museum of Science
Tony	86" (7'2")	Boston Museum of Science
Bambi	94" (7'10")	Boston Museum of Science
Bob	54" (4'6")	Boston Museum of Science
Tiger	79" (6'7")	Boston Museum of Science
Saulette	108" (9'0")	Franklin Park Children's Zoo
Jake	114" (9'6")	Franklin Park Children's Zoo
Bella	84" (7'0")	Worcester Science Center
Floyd	72" (6'0")	Worcester Science Center
Boa	54" (4'6")	Worcester Science Center
Lady	96" (8'0")	Earlham College
Sleeper	72" (6'0")	Boston University
Malcolm	80" (6'8")	Science Museum of Connecticut
Godzilla	93" (7'9")	Science Museum of Connecticut
Alexis	72" (6'0")	Science Museum of Connecticut
Julius	64" (5'4")	Science Museum of Connecticut
unnamed	63" (5'3")	Busch Gardens
unnamed	78" (6'6")	Busch Gardens

[Source: Boston Museum of Science; Franklin Park Children's Zoo, Boston; Worcester Science Center, Worcester, MA; Earlham College, Richmond, IN; Boston University; Science Museum of Connecticut, Hartford, CT; and Busch Gardens, Tampa, FL. Lengths given by the Worcester Science Center and Boston University are estimates. Data collected in 1989.]

Mystery Data C (Student Sheet 6)

These values are the lengths at birth of a group of 14 babies born at Mount Auburn Hospital in Cambridge, Massachusetts, in late August 1989.

[Source: Community Relations Department, Mount Auburn Hospital, Cambridge, MA.]

Looking at Mystery Data (Student Sheet 7)

These values are the heights of 11 trees in the United States, each of which reached a record-breaking height for its species. (We might consider these the "Tree All-Stars.")

Kind of Tree	Height
California redwood	4392 inches (366 feet)
Douglas fir	3624 inches (302 feet)
Noble fir	3336 inches (278 feet)
Giant sequoia	3264 inches (272 feet)
Ponderosa pine	2676 inches (223 feet)
Cedar	2628 inches (219 feet)
Sitka spruce	2592 inches (216 feet)
Western larch	2124 inches (177 feet)
Hemlock	1956 inches (163 feet)
Beech	1932 inches (161 feet)
Black cottonwood	1764 inches (147 feet)

[Source: The Diagram Group, *Comparisons.* New York: St. Martin's Press, 1980, p. 59.]

The heights are given in inches on Student Sheet 7 so that students will have a chance to work with large numbers and to compare these numbers with the values given in inches in the other Mystery Data sets. Calculators should be available so that students can easily change inches to feet as they try to estimate and visualize these heights.

Do any of these species grow in your community? If so, students might try to find a number of trees of a particular species and estimate their heights. Is the typical height they find for this species quite different from the record-breaking height? Developing strategies for estimating the height of a tree will involve students in a challenging mathematical problem.

Visualizing Measurement Data

Here, students are discussing Mystery Data A (p. 34) as they try to use what they know about their own heights to get a sense of what the mystery numbers might represent.

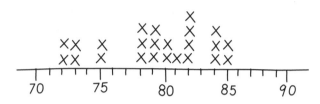

So you've told me a lot about the shape of these data. But what about these measurements? About how long or tall are these things?

Rebecca: They're taller than we are.

How do you know that?

Teresa: Well, I'm 52 inches tall and the shortest one is 72, so that's a lot taller than me.

The shortest is 72 inches? About how tall is that? Who has an estimate?

Pinsuba: It's as tall as you.

Nadim: It's as tall as my Dad.

Tuong: It's about up to the doorway.

Who has a way we can get a good estimate of how big 72 inches is?

Kenyana: We could measure it.

Yes, we could, and we can do that in a minute. But is there any way we can get a good estimate just by imagining about how big 72 inches is?

Vanessa: I have a way. If Teresa is 52 inches, then 72 inches is 20 inches taller than her. She can stand up, and then we can just show about 20 inches taller.

How would you show about 20 inches taller? Who has an idea?

DeShane: That's close to two feet, so we could put two rulers in a line over her head and that would be close.

David: Also, 72 inches is the same as 6 feet.

The same as 6 feet. How would that help?

Ahmad: Well, if we knew something that was 6 feet, then we could tell 72 inches.

Anyone know what might be 6 feet?

Kim: If we knew how tall the doorway is, that might be close.

Lina Li: Six feet is two yardsticks.

Tyrone: My dad's exactly 6 feet, and there's still about that much space [*showing with hands*] between him and the doorway.

So the smallest thing is about as tall as your dad, about up to here? What about the biggest—how big is 88 inches?

Finding the Median

What Happens

Materials

- '93 All-Star cards
- Student Sheet 4 (from Session 4, optional)
- Student Sheet 8 (1 per student, homework)
- Data collected in previous investigations
- Interlocking cubes, counting chips, or other concrete materials
- Unlined paper
- Graph paper

Students are introduced to the median as a formal measure that statisticians use to summarize a set of data. The median is one important landmark in data sets. Students find the median height for the class. They find the median height of the '93 NBA All-Stars and compare it with the median height of the class. They find the medians for the data they collected in earlier investigations. Student work focuses on:

- understanding that the median is the exact middle of the data when all the data are put in order

- finding the median in a set of data stretched out in a line (e.g., when the students line up in order by height)

- finding the median in a set of data that is grouped by frequency (e.g., on a line plot or other graph)

- understanding that the median is only one landmark in the data

- using the median to compare two data sets

In the investigation about heights, when you decided how much taller a fourth grader is than a first grader, you figured out ways to decide how tall a typical first grader or a typical fourth grader is. How did you pick one number or a few numbers to describe a group with so many different heights?

Finding the Median Height for This Class

Allow students to briefly describe some of the methods they used.

I'm going to show you a method that statisticians use when they are describing data. They find a landmark number called the median. *Median* means "middle." The *median* is the exact middle of the data when all the data are put in order.

If students have already come up with this method during previous investigations, point out that they invented this for themselves, just the way a mathematician once invented it. See the **Teacher Note,** Finding and Using the Median (p. 42).

Finding Our Median Height Ask students what they think the median height would be for the class. Students offer suggestions and methods they could use to be sure of their answer. To check, they line up in order of height. To find the middle, students might sit down in pairs—one from the short end, one from the tall end—until only one or two students are left.

If students suggested other strategies for finding the middle student, try one or two of their ideas.

If you have an odd number of students, the median is the height of the middle student. If you have an even number of students, you will have two students left in the middle. Ask students how they could decide what the middle value is. Explain that when the median was invented, statisticians decided that the "official" method when there are an even number of values would be to find the value midway between the two middle pieces of data.

Is the median value, the middle height, about what we said was a typical height for our class?

Thinking About the Median   Students compare the median with the ways they summarized the height data for the class. Usually the median will be a pretty good indicator of typical height for the class.

The median gives us some important information—that half the data is above and half the data is below that number. Our median height is [58 inches]. But what *doesn't* the median tell you about the data?

The students brainstorm this topic. They might think about it this way: If another class knew only their median height, what wouldn't they know? They wouldn't know the range of the data, and they wouldn't know how spread out or close together the data are. They wouldn't know where the clumps are, or if there are any really unusual values in the data. Could there be another class with the same median height that would look quite different when the students lined up in order? Let students try to describe such a situation. Guide them toward the conclusion that the median provides one important landmark, but doesn't give a complete picture.

Activity

What's the Median Height of the All-Stars?

Distribute the '93 All-Star cards randomly, one to a student, so the order of students' heights does not correspond to the order of the heights given on the cards.

Now those of you with cards are going to line up in an order that will let us find the median height of the '93 All-Star basketball teams.

Students line up according to the heights on their cards. They may use the pairing-off method described above or some other method suggested by students to find the median height. Since there are 24 players on the All-Star teams, students will have to find the value exactly between the two middle players.

Using the Median to Compare Data Sets   Once students have found the specific median height for the All-Stars, introduce a more general discussion of the median.

So now you know how to find a median. But what is a median good for? Why would anyone want to find a median?

Allow enough time for students to think hard about this. Looking at their copies of Student Sheet 4, the graphs of the All-Star players' heights, may help students see the median in the context of the whole data set. See also the **Dialogue Box,** What Good Is Knowing the Median? (p. 44).

One important use of the median is to compare sets of data. For example, you know that the median height for our class is [58 inches] and the median height of the '93 All-Stars is 79½ inches. How can we use this information to compare the heights of our class and the All-Stars?

Take students' suggestions. Remind students that they have already compared two sets of heights—theirs and the first graders'. Can they use similar methods now?

Finding the Median for Previously Collected Data Sets   In small groups, students find the median for the various data they collected previously—the raisin data, the family-size data, and the data on brothers and sisters. Each group starts with one data set. (More than one group can work on the same data.) Urge students to invent ways to find the middle for each data set in some concrete, physical way. Here are some possibilities:

■ For the raisin data: Use the collection of raisin boxes you saved with the number of raisins written inside the lids. Line up the boxes themselves and find the middle box. Or, use concrete materials such as interlocking cubes or counting chips.

■ For the family-size data and the data about brothers and sisters: Use interlocking cubes to build a tower to represent each family in the class; line up the towers in order of height and find the middle tower.

Once students have identified the median, they make a bar graph or line plot of the data and show where the median is. Although students have already plotted these data during previous investigations, they need to do it again so that they begin to see how to find a median on a graph that does not show all the individual values lined up in a row.

Session 5 Follow-Up

How Many Cavities?   Send home Student Sheet 8, which asks students to find out how many cavities they have had. They will use the data in class in the next couple of days.

 **Homework**

Finding and Using the Median

The median is an important landmark in a set of data. It is an average or a measure of center that helps summarize how the data are distributed. The median is the midpoint of the data set. If all the pieces of data are lined up in order, and one person counts from one end while another person counts from the other end, the value where they meet is the median value. If there is an odd number of pieces of data, the median is the value of the middle piece. If there is an even number of pieces of data, the median is the value midway between the two middle pieces.

According to the U.S. Bureau of Census, the median age in the United States in 1990 was 32.9 years. This statistic indicates that half the U.S. population was 32.9 years old or younger, while the remaining half of the population ranged in age from 32.9 years to the oldest living age. In other words, there are approximately as many people in the first three decades of life (0–30) as in the last, say, six decades of life (30–90).

Notice that the median is not the middle of the range of the data; if the range of the data is from 0 to 90 years, the middle of the range would be 45 years. But the population is not spread symmetrically over this range. Just as many people are in the first third of the range as in the last two-thirds, so the median—the value that equally divides the data set—is at age 30 rather than 45.

Another example, which the students explore in the next session, is this data set:

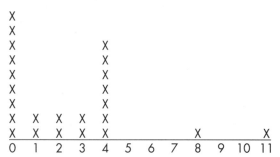

[Source: Dr. George W. McEachern III, DMD, Cambridge, MA.]

This line plot shows the number of lifetime cavities of twenty-four 9- to 12-year-olds.

While the middle of the range is 5.5 (halfway between 0 and 11), the median is 2. Knowing that the range is 0 to 11 and that the median is 2 tells us that there are as many children in the group with 0 to 2 cavities as there are children with 2 to 11 cavities.

Below is a line plot showing the number of raisins in 15 boxes, similar to those made in the first investigation in this unit.

```
                               X   X
                               X   X
                       X       X   X
                       X       X   X
            X          X   X   X   X
   28  29  30  31  32  33  34  35  36  37  38
```

To find the median, imagine that we take all the values from the line plot and stretch them out in order:

30 35 35 35 36 37 37 37 37 37 38 38 38 38 38
⬆
median = 37

The middle value is 37, so the median is 37 for this set of data. If the data set had contained one more box of 35 raisins, it would have looked like this:

30 35 35 35 35 36 37 37 37 37 37 38 38 38 38 38
⬆
median = 37

In this case, the median is between the two middle values; however, since the two middle values are the same, the median is still 37.

When the two middle values are not the same, as in the following data sets, the median is the value midway between the two middle numbers:

32 33 33 34 35 35 35 35 36 37 37 37 37 37 38 38
⬆
median = 35.5

32 33 33 34 35 35 35 35 37 37 37 37 37 38 38
⬆
median = 36

The following set of data (a survey of students' pets taken in a classroom in California) does not have a median.

```
        Dog  √ √ √ √ √ √ √ √ √ √ √ √ √
        Cat  √ √ √ √ √ √ √ √ √ √
       Fish  √ √ √ √ √ √
       Bird  √ √ √ √
    Hamster  √ √ √
      Mouse  √ √ √
      Horse  √ √ √
     Turtle  √ √
     Rabbit  √
 Guinea pig  √
      Snake  √
```

While we can order these categories in different ways (in alphabetical order, from most to least items, by size or weight), there is no intrinsic order to the items in the data set. When we line up the raisin data in order, we know that all the 35's always come after all the 34's and before the 36's. If we are finding the median height of students in a class, the students know how to line up according to height; 58 inches is always taller than 57 inches. But fish does not necessarily come before or after dog. If we had pictures of all the animals in the pet data, lining up the pictures and finding the middle one would not tell us anything about the data set. (Categorical data and the mode are addressed in the grade 4 Data and Fractions unit, *Three out of Four Like Spaghetti*.)

The median provides one landmark in the data, but it does not reveal all the important features of the data. The fact that the median age in the United States is 32.9 years gives us some information about the shape of these data because we bring some knowledge and experience to the subject. That is, we know that ages range from birth to somewhere in the nineties or the low hundreds. We know that very few people reach ages beyond 90. So we can imagine to some extent what the age data look like. However, we still do not know, for example, what proportion of the 30-and-over group is over 65, or how many of the 0–30 group are in their teens. Experience with and knowledge of the context will help us interpret a statistic such as the median. But for a data set to which we bring less knowledge, the median, or any other average, taken by itself, may not illuminate important aspects of the data.

D I A L O G U E B O X

What Good Is Knowing the Median?

Following is a discussion that occurred during the Session 5 activity Finding the Median Height for This Class (p. 39). This class is working to reach some understanding of the median of a data set.

So you know how to find a median. But what good is knowing the median? Why do you think statisticians or other scientists are interested in knowing the median of a set of data?

Alex: It's the middle number.

Yes, it is the middle number; for example, the middle height in our class is 58 inches. But if you knew that the median height of some other class was 58 inches, too, what would you know about that other class?

Sarah: Well, if they lined up, the middle kid would be 58 inches tall.

Uh-huh, what else?

Nhat: I don't agree with Sarah, because it might not be the middle kid. It might be between the two kids in the middle.

OK, so you're both saying that 58 inches is the middle value either way. How does that help us know something about the height of the class?

Shoshana: You know that half the kids are below 58 and half the kids are taller.

Qi Sun: They're like our class, about the same height.

They're like our class—what does that mean?

Qi Sun: The middle of their heights is 58 inches and so is ours.

What else could you say about whether they're like us or not?

Kyle: They wouldn't have to be exactly alike. They could have some kids who were much taller than kids in our class.

How would that work?

Kyle: The middle kid could still be 58 inches, but the kids taller than 58 inches could reach all the way up to 80 inches.

So the top half could be more spread out. What do other people think?

Sarah: I don't think it would be that spread out. Fifth graders aren't 80 inches tall.

Others: Yeah, that's silly. That's as tall as a basketball player.

So you're saying that you have some experience that tells you that another class with a median height of 58 inches wouldn't be as drastically different from ours as Kyle was saying. What do you think, Kyle?

Kyle: They probably wouldn't be all the way up to 80 inches, but there still could be some kids who would be taller.

Karen: Yeah, or shorter.

In this dialogue, the teacher attempts to move the students away from how to find the median to an explanation of what the median is good for—what it does and does not tell about the data it represents. Students need to be able not only to find a median, but also to interpret it.

Using Landmarks in Data

What Happens

Students examine another set of mystery data, describe the landmarks (such as the median, outliers, and clusters), and establish what the data represent. They use the median to compare the weights of cats and lions. They investigate the question: Who has more cavities, the Massachusetts group (Student Sheet 11) or our class? Student work focuses on:

- organizing data
- finding the median
- using the median to compare two sets of data

Materials

- Student Sheet 8 (from Session 5)
- Student Sheet 9 (1 per student)
- Student Sheet 10 (1 per student)
- Student Sheet 11 (1 per student)
- Unlined paper
- Calculators

Activity

Organizing Data and Finding the Median

Distribute Student Sheet 9, Cat Weights, which presents data for 24 domestic cats. Have students work in groups to organize the data in a graph or plot, write down as many important landmarks (e.g., the median, outliers, clusters, gaps) as they can see, and write a brief description based on these landmarks of the weights of the cats. Ask each group to find the median (if they don't do so on their own) and to decide if the median is a good description of the typical cat in this group. Be on the alert for difficulties students have in finding the median from a graph, as described in the **Dialogue Box,** Common Misconceptions About the Median ... and How to Help (p. 47).

❖ **Tip for the Linguistically Diverse Classroom** Pair students so that those not yet writing in English will have help in creating a brief description of the data on cat weights. Students might invent ways to visually highlight important features of the data on their graph or plot.

Activity

Another Mystery Data Set

Give out copies of Student Sheet 10, Another Mystery. Working with the whole class, give the students time to say everything they can about these data—clusters, clumps, gaps, the range, and so forth. Play Twenty Questions to establish what the data are. Information about the data set is presented in the **Teacher Note,** About the Data on Student Sheets 9–11 (p. 49).

Using the Median to Compare Cats and Lions Working in pairs or small groups, students find the median of the data on Student Sheet 10 and then use the median lion and cat weights to answer the question "About how many typical cats would it take to balance a typical lion?" Calculators should be available. If time permits, students can describe the strategies they used to answer the question.

Assessment

Who Has More Cavities?

Give out copies of Student Sheet 11, Cavity Data.

Here are some data that a dentist in Massachusetts collected about some of his 9- to 12-year-old patients. What can you say about these data?

After some discussion, ask students to find the median for these data. Observe the students as they work. Are they all able to find the median for a set of organized data? Ask students what the median tells them about the data.

We're going to find out how our class compares to this group. Have we had more, fewer, or about the same number of cavities as this group?

Using the completed homework sheets (Student Sheet 8) from Session 5, record on the board the number of cavities for each student. Ask students to make a line plot of the class data and find the median so they can compare the shape of the two data sets. If some students do not know exactly how many cavities they have had, they may estimate.

As you walk around the room observing, be aware of how students are working. Are all students able to organize the data and make a line plot? Have they looked at the range of the data to know an appropriate length for the line plot? Do they include in-between values for which there are no data on the line plot? Are some students using the line plot on Student Sheet 11 to assist them? Are they able to find the median for the class data?

How would you compare our class to this group? Does the median help? Does it tell you enough? What else would you want to say?

Encourage students to use the median for comparison, but also to look carefully at what the median shows and to add information that will provide a context for the median. Now is the time to nip in the bud any tendency to give a rote response simply because a formal measure has been introduced.

You might hear, for example, "Our median is 4; their median is 2; the difference is 2." This kind of response can obscure interesting features of the data. A richer description might be, "Our median is higher, so as a group we had more cavities; we had a lot more people with 5, 6, and 7 cavities, and we only had 5 people with no cavities." See the **Dialogue Box**, How Many Cavities Do We Have? (p. 48).

Following this discussion, ask the students to work individually to write descriptions of their work with the two sets of cavity data, titled "What we did" and "What we found out." This could be done in separate paragraphs or in two side-by-side columns. Collect the students' work.

Articulating what they did and what they found out, whether orally or in writing, is difficult for many students. Are students able to describe their work process clearly? Do they simply parrot back what they've heard others say? Are they able to express their ideas more clearly orally or in writing? You may wish to save their work in a portfolio.

Common Misconceptions About the Median ... and How to Help

While the idea of "middle" seems straightforward and easy to understand, the median can nevertheless be a difficult and complicated concept. As students encounter new examples, they may become confused about which "middle" they are trying to find.

Misconceptions may surface when students develop a graph of cat weights (Student Sheet 9). For example, students may say that the median is the middle of the horizontal axis, rather than the middle piece of data. Sometimes students find the "middle" without putting the data in order first. Perhaps the most common student misconception is that the median is the middle of the *range* of the data.

Emilio: We said the typical cat is 12½ pounds because 12½ is exactly in the middle.

How do you know that's the middle of the cat weights?

Emilio: Because the smallest is 7 and the fattest is 18 pounds, so they're 11 apart.

Marci: And 5½ is half of 11, so if you add 5½ to 7, that's 12½ . So 12½ is the exact middle between 7 and 18.

How would that work if we actually had all 24 cats here and we lined them up in order of weight?

Shiro: Um, well, the middle cat would be 12½ pounds.

Emilio: Oh ... no, it wouldn't ... I don't think we found exactly the middle cat.

Find some way to show how you'd line up all the cats according to weight and which would be the middle cat exactly. I'll check back with you in a few minutes.

It may take repeated experiences with these ideas for students to develop a firm grasp of the concept of median.

How Many Cavities Do We Have?

During the Assessment activity, Who Has More Cavities? (p. 46), students are looking at their own cavity data and comparing it to that given on Student Sheet 11.

Cavities in Our Class

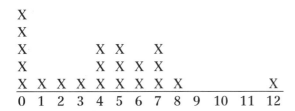

Joey: Our median is 4 and theirs is 2.

What do you think that tells us about comparing the number of cavities we have to the number they have?

Joey: We had 2 more?

What do you mean, 2 more? Anyone have an idea?

Luisa: Well, our middle person had 2 more cavities than their middle person.

Rebecca: It's like on the average we had more cavities.

Can anyone add to that? What if you were reporting on this research about cavities?

Kyle: If we use one kind of toothpaste and they use another, then we could say their kind was better.

Jesse: Yeah, or maybe we don't go to the dentist as much as they do.

Lesley Ann: Or we eat more junk food.

So you have a few theories about why we have more cavities than they do. We don't know if those theories are correct, but you all seem to agree that typically we have more cavities as a group than the Massachusetts group. The median helps us see the difference. What else is the same or different about our data and their data that the median doesn't tell you?

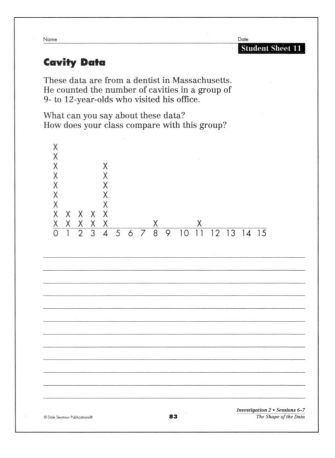

Rashaida: Nobody had more than 12 cavities in both groups.

What do you think about that? Does that surprise you?

Rashaida: You might think that we'd have people who had lots more cavities than their top person, but we didn't.

David: But even though we didn't have anyone higher than 12, they have more 1's, 2's, 3's, and 4's than we do. We had more 5's, 6's, and 7's.

Kenyana: And they had more people who didn't have any cavities.

Nick: Yeah, we only had 5 people with no cavities.

Do you think that's unusual for a group of kids your age? What do you think about that?

About the Data on Student Sheets 9–11

Student Sheet 9

The cats represented on Student Sheet 9 were unscientifically selected by the authors of this unit. They include Susan Jo's cat, Alexander; Rebecca's cats, Strawberry and Lady Jane Grey; and Andee's cat, Harmony. Other cats belong to colleagues and friends, and some data were collected at a local cat show. The cats were weighed and measured by the authors or by their owners.

Student Sheet 10

The mystery data on Student Sheet 10 are the weights of lions in a number of U.S. zoos. Their names and weights are shown in the table that follows. The four "no names" were in a litter of 4-month-old cubs in the Miami Zoo. The two heavier cubs in the litter are males and the two lighter cubs are females.

Toza	460 pounds
K.C.	453 pounds
Firecracker	450 pounds
Charlie	432 pounds
Valentino	420 pounds
Linda	402 pounds
Mimi	400 pounds
Sunshire	378 pounds
Zike	350 pounds
Gilbert	325 pounds
Webster	325 pounds
Kimba	307 pounds
Gira	302 pounds
Alice	300 pounds
Rex	290 pounds
China	289 pounds
Hannah	280 pounds
Asha	240 pounds
Basra	212 pounds
No name 1	105 pounds
No name 2	100 pounds
No name 3	45 pounds
No name 4	41 pounds

[Source: Zoos in Atlanta, Cleveland, Little Rock, Memphis, Miami, The Bronx, Philadelphia, Rochester, San Antonio, and Washington, D.C. Data collected in 1987.]

Student Sheet 11

The cavity data on Student Sheet 11 come from the 9- to 12-year olds who visited a pediatric dentist in Cambridge, MA, during about two weeks in August 1989. The dentist reports that urban children typically have more cavities than children from nonurban areas because they have easier access to junk food. The ages and number of cavities of the children in the data are shown below.

0 cavities	1 9-year-old
	4 10-year-olds
	2 11-year-olds
	2 12-year-olds
1 cavity	1 10-year-old
	1 11-year-old
2 cavities	1 10-year-old
	1 12-year-old
3 cavities	2 10-year-olds
4 cavities	4 11-year-olds
	3 12-year-olds
8 cavities	1 11-year-old
11 cavities	1 12-year-old

[Source: Dr. George W. McEachern III, DMD, Cambridge, MA.]

INVESTIGATION 3

A Data Project: Investigating Sleep

What Happens

Sessions 1 and 2: What Do We Want to Find Out? Students' work in this unit culminates with a more extended investigation in data analysis. Students discuss possibilities for data they might collect about sleep. They divide into small research teams and choose a question to investigate. Teams collect preliminary data and interpret it. They then confer with the teacher and make decisions about improving their research for the final investigation.

Sessions 3, 4, and 5: The Research Team at Work Students conduct their final investigation, collecting data and representing the data in several ways. The research teams put their analysis into publishable form as a written report, a class presentation, a display, or a letter to the principal or parents about their findings.

Mathematical Emphasis

- Undertaking a complete data analysis project, from defining a question to publishing results
- Carrying out all the stages of a data analysis investigation
- Choosing and refining a research question
- Viewing the data in several different ways, using quick sketches and other representations to organize and display the data

What to Plan Ahead of Time

Materials

- Materials for making sketch graphs and initial representations, including plain paper, graph paper, interlocking cubes, counting materials, and optional stick-on notes for making and modifying rough draft graphs (Sessions 1–5)
- Overhead projector (Sessions 1–2)
- Materials for publishing findings, including a variety of paper, scissors, glue, and crayons or colored markers (Sessions 3–5)

Other Preparation

Duplicate student sheets and teaching resources (located at the end of this unit) as follows. If you have Student Activity Booklets, copy only the item marked with an asterisk.

For Sessions 1–2

Student Sheet 12, Three Nights' Sleep (p. 87): 1 per student (homework)

Sleep Table* (p. 90): 1 transparency

For Sessions 3–5

Student Sheet 13, Wake Up! (p. 88): 1 per student (homework)

Student Sheet 14, Representing How People Wake Up (p. 89): 1 per student (homework)

KEY

Red = room 10
Blue = room 9

There is a huge bump
from 10½ to 11.
The range is from
8½ to 13½.
The median was 11.
The typical hours of
sleep are 11 hrs.
The mode is 11 hrs.
because 17 out of
45 first graders
were at that number.

8½ 9½ 10½ 11½ 12½ 13½ 14½
Hours of Sleep

What Do We Want to Find Out?

What Happens

Students discuss possibilities for data they might collect about sleep. They divide into small research teams and choose a question to investigate. Teams collect preliminary data and interpret it. They then confer with the teacher and make decisions about improving their research for the final investigation. Student work focuses on:

- planning an extended investigation
- choosing and refining an investigation question
- collecting, recording, organizing, describing, and interpreting preliminary data
- refining and improving research strategies

Materials

- Transparency of sleep table
- Materials for making sketch graphs and initial representations, optional stick-on notes
- Overhead projector
- Student Sheet 12 (1 per student, homework)
- Calculators

 Ten-Minute Math: Broken Calculator   During the next few days, take short periods of time outside the math hour to do Broken Calculator problems.

Pose the problem.

Make 100 without using a 1 or a 0.

Students solve the problem by themselves. Encourage them to use various operations.

Record their solutions on the board. For example, 4×25, $52 + 48$, $322 - 222$. Keep them on the board while you present the next problem.

Make 1000 without using a 1 or a 0.

Have students share their solutions.

Ask the students:

Were you able to use the solutions for making 100 to help find solutions for making 1000? Which solutions for 100 were easy to change for 1000, and which were difficult? Why?

A Note About the Final Project

This project gives students the chance to carry out an extended investigation of data, from posing the initial question through publication of results. Virtually every schoolchild has already confronted issues about sleep: When do I have to go to bed? How much sleep do I need? Under what circumstances can I stay up late? These topics are often the basis for vigorous discussions between children and those responsible for their bedtimes. Because it is essential that students pursue questions and issues of particular interest to them within the general topic area, it is impossible to predict exactly what directions this investigation may take. The following sessions suggest an appropriate process, but the particular ideas to be investigated will emerge from your students.

Data collection can usually be done outside of class time, but students visiting other classrooms may need help arranging visits. Since the students will be working in research teams, much of their time will be spent in small-group activities. The teams may proceed at different paces and will probably need periodic conferences with you about their progress.

How Long Do People Sleep?

Put on the overhead projector the transparency for the sleep table, How Many Hours Do People Sleep? This table presents information about the amount of sleep people get at different ages.

Notice that data points on this list are in decimals. Make sure your students understand in general the form of decimals and the meaning of numbers to the right of the decimal point. Review the fact that $0.5 = \frac{1}{2}$. Discuss the meaning of numbers such as 9.8 (a little less than 10) and 8.1 (a little more than 8). Students should understand, for example, how to compare 7.2 with 7.0 and 9.6 with 10.2.

Here are some data collected by a group of scientists who do research about sleep. They show how much sleep people at different ages typically get each night. What do you notice about these data? ... What else do you notice?

Encourage students to describe the data as completely as possible. Call attention to the data for their age group: Do they think it's accurate for their class?

A Quick Survey Explain that students are going to take a quick survey of how much sleep the people in their class typically get.

How should we begin to get that information?

Students will need to consider what a typical night is. Should they choose last night? Are they considering a school night or a weekend night? Are they going to say how much sleep they are "supposed" to get, or will they figure out how much they actually do get? If someone lies awake for a while at night, how should the bedtime be figured? If someone usually turns over and goes back to sleep for half an hour after the alarm goes off, does that half hour count? Help students arrive at a consensus definition of a typical night's sleep.

Calculating Number of Sleep Hours   Students work together in pairs or groups of three to figure out the number of hours of sleep each person in the group gets.

While students likely know their bedtimes and when they get up, they may never have thought about the actual number of hours they sleep. Some students may have difficulty figuring out the number. If this occurs, have students share several methods they use for determining sleep duration.

Record all the students' data on a line plot displayed where everyone can see it.

What would you say about our data? How does our class data compare with the research data about your age group?

Discussing Issues About Sleep   After some discussion of the class data, introduce the students' research project:

We're going to do a study of sleep patterns in this school. In a few minutes, we're going to break into research groups so you can decide on particular questions you want to investigate. But before we do that, let's take a few minutes to talk about sleep.

Encourage students to discuss sleep, giving personal examples that involve themselves, siblings, or friends. You might raise the following questions during this discussion: Do you think you get enough sleep? Do you think most people your age get enough sleep? Do you have arguments with your parents about sleep? How much sleep do you think you need? Do you think it's about the same for everyone your age? What about your younger or older brothers and sisters?

Allow this discussion to continue until you feel that students have raised most of the issues, as this will give them a good start toward choosing a research question.

Let's brainstorm some questions that we might be able to investigate about sleep by collecting data ourselves. Questions might occur to you as you look at the research data, as you look at our own data on the line plot, or as you think about the discussion we just had. I'll list the questions as you come up with them.

At this point, list all suggested questions. Don't attempt to edit students' ideas, even though they may be impractical. Part of their job as researchers will be to devise and refine a question for which they can easily collect data. See the **Teacher Note,** I Wanna Do It Myself! (p. 57).

Activity

Choosing a Question

Divide the class into small research teams of three or four who will work together for the duration of the investigation. Their first task as a team is to choose a question they want to investigate. They might choose one from the list made by the class or, as they talk, they may think of something else that interests them. A question involving comparison (for example, of first and sixth graders, of students in this school and another school, of boys and girls) would provide an appropriate challenge for students who have done the other investigations in this unit.

❖ **Tip for the Linguistically Diverse Classroom** Research teams should mix students with varying degrees of proficiency in English. As students are pondering questions, encourage everyone in the group to use visual aids, pointing, and quick sketches to ensure comprehension.

As each team comes up with a question, they should have a brief conference with you about their idea. Your role is to help them refine their question, to encourage them to include some kind of comparison in their investigation, and to refer them to resources for further refining their questions. Try not to simplify a question at this time, even if you see that a group will have trouble with their investigation. Revising their questions will be part of the task of the research teams. See the **Dialogue Box,** Helping Students Refine Their Questions (p. 58).

After the teams have checked in with you, each group should continue to work on refining their question and deciding what data they need to collect.

Here are some of the questions that student teams have selected:

- Do first graders get more sleep than students our age?
- Are there some students at each grade level who stay up much later than others?
- Do boys and girls have the same weekend bedtimes?
- Do the oldest students in the school get the least sleep?
- What's the typical weekend bedtime for each grade level?

Don't worry if some questions overlap. Different perspectives on the same topic can add to the richness of what students learn.

Working with Preliminary Data

Each team collects, records, organizes, and describes some initial data that they think will help answer their question. Emphasize to students that these data are preliminary, a first try to get some information to help them plan their study; they will collect more data later on.

Suppose the question is, "Do boys and girls have the same weekend bedtimes?" The team could start by taking a survey in their own classroom to find each student's bedtime last Friday and Saturday.

Once they collect their data, the research teams find a way to organize it. Encourage them to be clear and accurate without taking time to create a polished product at this point. Students then write a description of what they think the data show, and develop some theories about the patterns in their data.

❖ **Tip for the Linguistically Diverse Classroom**   After groups have completed their surveys, English-proficient students can write the descriptions of the data, as well as the group's theories about certain patterns; other students can provide sketch graphs or other visual representations.

For example, one team investigated girls' and boys' Friday bedtimes. They found that the median bedtime for boys was an hour and a half later than the median bedtime for girls! They came up with several theories about their data: Boys eat more sugar than girls so they are more active and stay up later; boys are more demanding and don't give in to their parents when they are told to go to bed; girls get up earlier, too, so they actually get the same amount of sleep.

Taking a survey of about 20 people (in their classroom, on the school bus, or among their friends) is a good way for students to collect their initial data. Later, they can collect data from a larger sample.

Bedtimes
- 🕗 8:00 ✓
- 🕣 8:30
- 🕘 9:00 ✓ ✓ ✓ ✓ ✓
- 🕤 9:30 ✓ ✓ ✓ ✓ ✓ ✓ ✓
- 🕙 10:00 ✓ ✓
- 🕥 10:30 ✓ ✓

Student's preliminary data collection

A Student-Teacher Conference   After each research team has completed a preliminary investigation, they again have a brief conference with you to help them decide what their final investigation will be.

Some students may have found that, because of the way they formulated their question, people interpreted it differently. Some may have found that younger students typically did not know the answer to the question. Some may have discovered that the data they collected did not help them answer their question. Or, they may have found that a more interesting question emerged from their data, one that they now want to pursue.

Some may have seen an interesting pattern in their data, as in the Friday bedtime example, but need to collect more data to see if the pattern really holds. The team that investigated boys' and girls' Friday bedtimes decided that they would also collect times students get up on Saturdays so they could compare the total amount of sleep for boys and girls.

Encourage students to examine critically both their question and their data and to come up with new strategies for improving their research.

Sessions 1 and 2 Follow-Up

Three Nights' Sleep   Student Sheet 12 asks students to keep a record of the number of hours they actually sleep for three consecutive nights. They also record notes about any special circumstances that affect the amount of sleep they get each night.

 **Homework**

I Wanna Do It Myself!

Teacher Note

When upper elementary students start their own projects in data collection and analysis, they often select questions that you can immediately recognize as problematic. It's very tempting to simplify their questions for them, to save them from wrestling with messy data or overwhelming amounts of information. Isn't it important to keep students from being overwhelmed? Shouldn't a teacher help simplify their questions in advance? The answer is no! The final projects may solicit messy data, but wrestling with messy data is an important part of the analytic process.

Students must struggle with these issues themselves, but teachers play an important role in the process. It is vital that you encourage students to take plenty of time to think about their research questions. What data would help them answer their questions? How can they get those data? After students have collected their data, they must—with your support—carefully consider their results. Are they reasonable? Can students see any patterns in the data? Are there other avenues to take? Messy data lie at the heart of the process—in fact, most real data are messy. Tidying them up too early will not help students in the long run.

Continued on next page

As an example, when students in one upper elementary class collected information about ways in which they had been injured while playing, they ended up with so much data that they could not easily organize and describe them. They concluded that they couldn't make any sense of their results unless they limited the sphere of their investigation. They decided to limit the study to play injuries at school. This more focused study allowed them to find patterns in the data, and they were ultimately able to make important recommendations about safety on their own playground. The students were able to make good decisions on their own about how to focus their study after their first experiences with their data—and they learned something important about data analysis in the process.

D I A L O G U E   B O X

Helping Students Refine Their Questions

During this discussion, the teacher asks a few key questions to help students focus the question they plan to investigate for their final project.

Kim: We're going to find out how much sleep a first grader gets.

How did you choose that idea? Why are you interested in that?

Alex: Well, we were talking about the little kids who stay up really late.

Tuong: Yeah, my friend's little sister stays up really late, even later than I go to bed.

Lina Li: And there's this kid Jonah from Mr. Weinberg's class who's always asleep on the bus going home.

B.J.: I had to go to bed at 7 o'clock when I was in first grade.

Rafael: You never went to bed at 7 o'clock. You used to stay up and watch T.V.

B.J.: Yeah, but that was Friday. On the school nights I had to go to bed at 7.

Are you wondering whether first graders stay up later than you did at that age?

Lina Li: Yeah. We think that a lot of the little kids stay up too late.

That would make an interesting comparison—how late kids in fourth grade stayed up when they were in first grade compared to how late first graders stay up now. Have bedtimes changed since you were in first grade?

Kim: We could ask kids in our class and ask all the first graders.

Lina Li: Yeah, but the first graders can't all tell time. They probably don't know.

Tuong: And some of them might just say they go to bed at 9 o'clock because they're bragging, but it might not really be true.

Maybe the first grade teachers would have some ideas about how you could find out the real times. I know that Ms. Cannelli has talked to me about how late some of her first graders go to bed on school nights, so I bet she'd be interested in talking to you about your idea. She might have information that would help you figure out exactly what to ask.

The Research Team at Work

What Happens

Students conduct their final investigation, collecting data and representing the data in several ways. The research teams put their analysis into publishable form as a written report, a class presentation, a display, or a letter to the principal or parents about their findings. Student work focuses on:

- carrying out an extended investigation
- representing data in several ways
- preparing a publication that includes a statement of the research question, a presentation graph, a written description of the data, and an interpretation of the findings

Materials

- Materials for making sketch graphs and initial representations
- A variety of paper, scissors, glue, and crayons or colored markers for final presentations
- Student Sheet 13 (1 per student, homework)
- Student Sheet 14 (1 per student, homework)

Research teams now undertake their final investigation. From this point, not all teams will go through exactly the same stages. Some may need to refine their questions and collect new data, while others may be satisfied with their question but need additional data. As needed, the research teams will do the following:

- Refine or change their question
- Decide on their final data-collection procedure
- Decide how to record their data
- Collect and record their data
- Organize and represent their data in several different ways
- Write a description of their data

You may need to help coordinate some of the data collection, especially if it involves gathering information from other classes. Check in with each team periodically. After the data are collected, encourage students to represent them in several different ways with sketch graphs or concrete materials (a line plot, bar graph, interlocking cubes, and so forth) so they can see different aspects of the data.

Activity

Collecting, Organizing, and Describing Data

Developing Theories and Publishing Findings

The final task of each research team is to put their analysis into publishable form. This may be a written report, a class presentation, a display, or a letter to the principal or to parents about their findings. These final results must include a statement of the research question, a presentation graph showing the data, a written description of the data, and the students' interpretation of their findings.

❖ **Tip for the Linguistically Diverse Classroom**   As in other situations, the publishing tasks can be divided to take into account proficiency in English; those who are comfortable writing can take primary responsibility for that part, while others contribute more to the visual presentation.

Interpretation includes students' hypotheses and theories about why the data look the way they do. Depending on the question, it could also include recommendations. For example, does it seem that about a third of the first graders are not getting enough sleep? Are too many students staying up late on Wednesday night because of a particular TV program? The researchers may have recommendations about these kinds of findings.

You may want students to display their reports and their data on the walls or on table tops before you start the presentations. This gives all the students an opportunity to observe what other groups have done and prepare questions to ask during the presentations.

Assessment

Group Presentations

As groups present their reports, encourage the rest of the students to think about questions they want to ask. Follow each presentation with a question-and-answer period.

You will get a lot of information about what students have learned in this unit throughout the final investigation. Observe the students as they work in teams choosing a question, analyzing the data, and preparing their reports; listen to their presentations and responses to questions; listen to the questions they ask other teams; and listen to their responses during the final discussion.

You may want to ask yourself the following questions: Were the students able to plan and complete a full data collection process, from deciding the question to the final report, in a sensible way? Were the students able to incorporate ideas from the unit into their process and report? Were they able to present their findings in a way that the other students could understand? For more detail, see the **Teacher Note,** Assessment: Group Presentations, (p. 62).

Conclude the project with a discussion in which students critique their investigation. You might ask: Were there limitations to your study? Were there aspects that did not satisfy you or that you might do differently next time? Are there now other questions you would ask?

One team, for example, was unsure that the data from the youngest students in their study were reliable; they thought the students might have exaggerated their bedtimes. Since there seemed to be no other practical way of learning the bedtimes of these students, some team members thought a different question might have been better. One team member wondered if the young students' teacher might have cooperated in sending a survey home, to get more reliable information from the parents.

Choosing Student Work to Save

As the unit ends, you may want to use one of the following options for creating a record of students' work on this unit.

■ Students look back through their folders or notebooks and write about what they learned in this unit, what they remember most, what was hard or easy for them. You might have students do this work during their writing time.

■ Students select one to two pieces of work as their best work, and you also choose one to two pieces of their work to be saved in a portfolio for the year. You might include students' written responses to the assessment, Who Has More Cavities? (Investigation 2, Session 7), and any other assessment tasks from this unit. Students can create a separate page with brief comments describing each piece of work.

■ You may want to send a selection of work home for parents to see. Students write a cover letter describing their work in this unit. This work should be returned if you are keeping a portfolio of mathematics work for each student.

Sessions 3, 4, and 5 Follow-Up

 **Homework**

Wake Up!   Student Sheet 13 asks students to collect data about methods that they and other people outside school use to wake up when they have to.

Representing How People Wake Up   Student Sheet 14 instructs students to organize and represent the data from Student Sheet 13 about how people wake up. Be sure to send home with each child the completed Student Sheet 13.

Assessing a group report is a complex process that can provide a wealth of information about students' understanding of data analysis. You need to consider how the group determined their question, how they collected the data, how they displayed the data, how valid were their conclusions, and how comprehensive was their report. In addition, you need to be sensitive to how the individual students contributed to the work, and how they worked with one another in making group decisions. The following example illustrates how one teacher interpreted and made sense of a group report from her class.

Irena, Nick, Vanessa, and Nadim were the members of the group that wanted to find out how much longer first graders sleep than fifth graders. The group worked in pairs, with one pair surveying the first grade and the other pair surveying the fifth grade. Each person surveyed half of a classroom, asking each student in turn, "What time do you go to bed? What time do you get up?" After returning to class, the group calculated the number of sleep hours for each student and determined the median for each grade.

Nick's data recording and calculating sheet on the next page shows some of their work. You may notice that there's an error in this record; the second amount should be 9½ hours instead of 10½. In this case, the error does not affect the median, and Nick's work as shown on the recording sheet is sound and logical.

Each person in the group prepared line plots for the students he or she had surveyed. (There were eight line plots, showing bedtimes and get-up times for both first graders and fifth graders, males and females. See p. 64 for the line plots for fifth graders.) The group then prepared their oral report, which included the following remarks.

Irena: We wanted to find out how much longer does a first grader sleep than a fifth grader. Nick and Vanessa went to the fifth grade. Nadim and I went to the first grade. I talked to the females and he talked to the males.

Nadim: Male first graders usually go to bed at 8:00 and wake up at 7:30.

Irena: Female first graders sleep two hours longer than fifth graders.

Nadim: And a male first grader sleeps two hours longer than a male fifth grader.

Irena: Males and females were the same.

Vanessa: Most fifth graders go to bed at 9:30 and get up at 7:00.

Nick: Male and females were the same, too.

By listening to their report and by making on-going observations of the group during their investigation, the teacher made the following assessment of the group's work. As with most assessments, these observations led to more questions:

The group focused on a specific research question and devised a way to collect the data so as to avoid duplication of efforts. They were able to organize the data and figure out the number of hours each student slept. Members in the group worked independently at times on a portion of the investigation, yet the group was able to pull all the data together to answer their research question to their own satisfaction.

However, it's not clear how the group reached their conclusion that first graders sleep two hours longer than fifth graders. Were the data really the same for males and females? How did they reach the conclusion that bedtime for first graders was 8:00 and wake-up time 7:30? Did they analyze the bedtimes separately from the wake-up times? Did they use their calculated number of sleep hours in their analysis?

Continued on next page

Nick

Median 9

5th graders (males)

9:30 - 630 √ 9 hours
930 - 700   10 and a half hours
1130 - 700 √ 9 and a half hours
12:30 - 600 √ 6 and a half hours
1000 - 600 √ 8 hours
930 - 630 √ 9 hours
930 - 630 √ 9 hours
1000 - 630 √ 8 and a half hours
930 - 630 √ 9 hours
930 - 700 √ 9 and a half hours
930 - 600 √ 8 and a half hours
930 - 700 √ 9 and a half hours
1000 - 700 √ 9 hours
1000 - 700 √ 9 hours

$6\frac{1}{2}$ $7\frac{1}{2}$ 8 $8\frac{1}{2}$ $8\frac{1}{2}$ 9 9 9 9 9 9 $9\frac{1}{2}$ $9\frac{1}{2}$ $10\frac{1}{2}$

Continued on next page

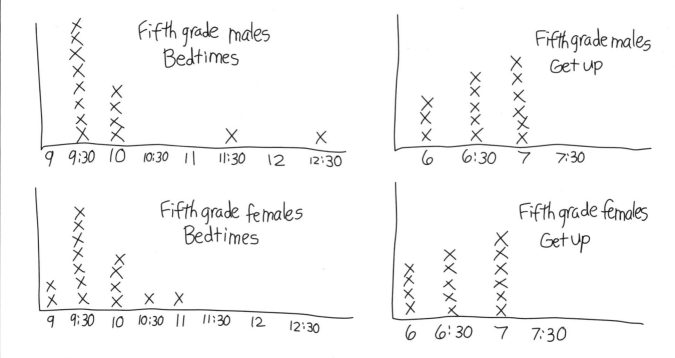

Following the group presentation, the teacher asked the rest of the class if they had any questions for the group. Some are below.

Teresa: Why did you split it up into male and female?

Irena: We did it because we might get mixed up. I might go to a person he already did.

DeShane: Why did you make separate line plots for what time you went to bed and what time you wake up? Why didn't you just do a line plot that showed how many hours they slept? Why didn't you just show 10 hours, 11 hours, and 12 hours?

Nadim: We thought if we did that people would think that you went to bed at 12:00. We figured out the number of hours kids slept on paper, but we didn't want to show that. We thought it would be easier for others to see the information the way we put it.

This question-and-answer period provided the teacher with additional information about the group and also about the understandings of other students in the class.

Irena's response to Teresa's question indicated that the group's reason for collecting male and female data might be more logistical rather than an inherent interest in whether the data would be different.

DeShane's question was a substantive one, focusing on the relationship of how the data were displayed to show the information the group wanted to convey. He wondered why the group had made line plots of the responses to their survey question—When do you go to bed and when do you get up?—rather than to their original research question, How much longer do first graders sleep than fifth graders? Nadim's response to his question indicated that the group might have actually discussed different ways of presenting the data, or as the teacher surmised, that Nadim was very quick at coming up with logical reasons, after the fact, for why things were done as they were.

Estimation and Number Sense

Basic Activity

Students mentally estimate the answer to an arithmetic problem that they see displayed for about a minute. They discuss their estimates. Then they find a precise solution to the problem by using mental computation strategies.

Estimation and Number Sense provides opportunities for students to develop strategies for mental computation and for judging the reasonableness of the results of a computation done on paper or with a calculator. Students focus on:

- looking at a problem as a whole
- reordering or combining numbers within a problem for easier computation
- looking at the largest part of each number first (looking at hundreds before tens, thousands before hundreds, and so forth)

Materials

Calculators (for variation)

Procedure

Step 1. Present a problem on the chalkboard or overhead. For example:

$$9 + 62 + 91 + 30$$

Step 2. Allow students to think about the problem for about a minute. Students come up with the best estimate they can for the solution. This solution may be, but does not have to be, an exact answer. Students do not write anything down or use the calculator during this time.

Step 3. Cover up the problem and have students discuss what they know. Ask questions such as the following: "What did you notice about the numbers in this problem? Did you estimate an answer? How did you make your estimate?"

Encourage all kinds of estimation statements and strategies. Some will be more general, some may be quite precise: "It's definitely bigger than 100 because I saw a 90 and a 60," "It has to be 192 because the 91 and the 9 make 100 and the 30 and the 62 make 92." Be sure that you con-

tinue to encourage a variety of observations, especially the "more than, less than" statements, even if some students have solved it exactly.

Step 4. Uncover the problem and continue the discussion. Ask students to consider further:

"What do you notice now? What do you think about your estimates? Do you want to change them? What are some mental strategies you can use to solve the problem exactly?"

Variations

Addition and Subtraction Problems That Require Reordering Give problems such as the following ones in which grouping the numbers in particular ways helps solve the problem more easily:

$$6 + 2 - 4 + 1 - 5 + 4 + 5 - 2$$

$$36 + 22 + 4 + 8$$

$$112 - 30 + 60 - 2$$

$$654 - 12 + 300 + 112$$

Encourage students to look at the problem as a whole before they start to solve it. Rather than using each number and operation in sequence, they see what numbers are easy to put together to give quick answers to part of the problem. Then they combine their partial results to solve the whole problem.

Problems with Large Numbers Present problems that require students to "think from left to right" and to round numbers to "nice numbers" in order to come up with a good estimate. For example:

$8 + 1200 + 130$	$\$3.15 \times 9$
$\$5.13$	$230 + 343 + 692$
$\$6.50$	
$+ \$3.30$	

Continued on next page

Present problems in both horizontal and vertical formats. If the vertical format triggers a rote procedure of starting from the right and "carrying," encourage students to look at the numbers as a whole, and to think about the largest parts of the numbers first. Thus, for the problem 230 + 343 + 692, they might think first, "About how much is 692?—700." Then, thinking in terms of the largest part of the numbers first (hundreds), they might reason: "300 and 700 is a thousand, and 200 more is 1200, and then there's some extra, so I think it's a little over 1200."

Fractions   Pose problems using fractions and ask students to estimate the number of wholes the result is closest to. Start by posing problems such as ½ + ¼ or ½ + ¾, and ask, "Is the answer more than or less than one?" Eventually, you can include fractions with larger results and expand the question to "Is the answer closer to 0, 1, or 2?" Begin to include problems such as 5 × ¼ and 3 × ⅛. Use fractions such as 9/4, 50/7, 100/26, or 63/20, and ask, "About how many wholes are in this fraction?"

Is It Bigger or Smaller?   Use any of the whole number problems suggested above, but pose a question such as those used for fractions to help students practice their estimation: Is this bigger than 20? Is it smaller than $10.00? If I have $20.00, do I have enough to buy these four things?"

Using the Calculator   The calculator can be used to check results. Emphasize that it is easy to make mistakes on a calculator. Sometimes you press the wrong number or the wrong operation. Sometimes you leave out a number, or a key sticks and doesn't register. However, people who are good at using the calculator always make a mental estimate so they can tell whether their result is reasonable. You can pose some problems like this one:

> I was adding 212, 357, and 436 on my calculator. The answer I got was 615. Was that a reasonable answer? Why not?

Include problems in which the result is reasonable and problems in which it is not. When the answer is unreasonable, some students may be interested in figuring out what happened. For example, in the above case, I accidentally punched in 46 instead of 436.

Related Homework Options

Problems with Many Numbers   Give one problem with many numbers that must be added and subtracted. Students show how they can reorder the numbers in the problem to make it easier to solve. They solve the problem using two different methods in order to double-check their solution. One method might be using the calculator. Here is an example of such a problem:

$$30 - 6 + 92 - 20 + 56 + 70 + 8$$

Broken Calculator

Basic Activity

Students work to get an answer on their calculator display while pretending that some of the keys are missing. The missing keys may be operations, numbers, or both. After students find one solution, they find others by making a small change in the first one. In this way, the solutions form a pattern.

Broken Calculator helps students develop flexibility in solving problems. They pull numbers apart and put them back together in a variety of ways as they look for expressions to substitute for given numbers. Students focus on:

- finding alternative paths to an answer when a familiar one isn't available
- finding many ways to get one answer
- writing related problems

Materials

Calculators

Procedure

Step 1. Pose the problem. For example, "I want to make 35 using my calculator, but the 3 key and the 5 key are broken. How can I use my calculator to do this task?"

Step 2. Students solve the problem by themselves. They record their solution in some way that another student can understand. Students in small groups check each other's solutions on their calculators.

Step 3. List some of the students' solutions on the board. Here are some possible solutions to making 35 without the 3 and 5 keys:

$$76 - 41 \qquad 29 + 6 \qquad 4 \times 9 - 1$$

Step 4. Students choose one solution and extend it, making a series of related solutions that follows a pattern. For example:

76 – 41	29 + 6	2 × 18 – 1
77 – 42	28 + 7	4 × 9 – 1
79 – 44	27 + 8	6 × 6 – 1
81 – 46	26 + 9	
82 – 47	24 + 11	

Students check each other's solutions and find another solution that follows the same pattern.

Variations

Restricting Number Keys

- Students make numbers without using the digits in those numbers, for example:

  Make 1000 without using a 1 or a 0.

  998 + 2

  997 + 3

  996 + 4

- Students make decimals without using the decimal point. Start with the simplest ones (0.1, 0.5, 0.25, 0.75, or 1.5) only after students have some experience relating them to fractions and division. You might start by providing a solution or two and challenge them to find some more: "I can make 0.5 on my calculator by using the keys 1 ÷ 2. Why do you think that works? Can you find another way to make 0.5?"

  Some solutions for making 0.5 are as follows:

2 ÷ 4	3 ÷ 6	4 ÷ 8
5 ÷ 10	100 ÷ 200	1000 ÷ 2000

Restricting Operation Keys

- Students make a number using only addition. If you suggest a large number, students can make use of landmark numbers. For example:

  Make 2754.

2000 + 700 + 54	2750 + 4	2749 + 5
2000 + 600 + 154	2751 + 3	2748 + 6

Continued on next page

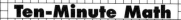

■ Students make a number using only subtraction. Present the challenge of getting a number on the display using only subtraction. The +, ×, and ÷ keys are broken. Patterns of solutions for making 8 might look like these:

20 – 12	1008 – 1000
19 – 11	908 – 900
18 – 10	808 – 800
17 – 9	708 – 700

■ Students make a number using only multiplication and division. The + and – keys are broken. Pick numbers that have many factors. Answers for making 24 might be:

1 × 24	24 ÷ 1	24 × 1 ÷ 1
2 × 12	48 ÷ 2	24 × 2 ÷ 2
3 × 8	72 ÷ 3	24 × 3 ÷ 3
4 × 6		24 × 4 ÷ 4

(One student filled a page with the third series so he could say he'd gotten the most answers.)

Restricting Both Operations and Digits

■ Make the missing operations problems more challenging by also not allowing students to use any of the digits in the final number. For example:

Make 654 using only addition and subtraction, and without using the digits 6, 5, or 4.

Related Homework Option

Pose one or two Broken Calculator problems only. Challenge students to solve the problems in more than one way, and to make their different solutions follow a pattern. They should write their solutions so that another student can read them and know what to do on the calculator.

If students do not have calculators at home, give them time to try out their solutions the next day in school.

The following activities will help ensure that this unit is comprehensible to students who are acquiring English as a second language. The suggested approach is based on *The Natural Approach: Language Acquisition in the Classroom* by Stephen D. Krashen and Tracy D. Terrell (Alemany Press, 1983). The intent is for second-language learners to acquire new vocabulary in an active, meaningful context.

Note that *acquiring* a word is different from *learning* a word. Depending on their level of proficiency, students may be able to comprehend a word upon hearing it during an investigation, without being able to say it. Other students may be able to use the word orally, but not read or write it. The goal is to help students naturally acquire targeted vocabulary at their present level of proficiency.

We suggest using these activites just before the related investigations. The activities can also be led by English-proficient students.

Investigation 1

family, people, children (kids)

1. Show several pictures of different families and identify the different members.

   There are four *people* in this *family*. Here are the parents. These are the *children*. Some people call their children *kids*.

2. Have the students draw a picture of their family. Ask them to look at their pictures in order to answer questions that can be answered with one-word responses.

   Whose family has more kids—Tuong's family or Emilio's family?

   How many people are in Nhat's family?

   How people are in Pinsuba's family?

Investigation 2

height, tall, pounds, weigh

1. Measure students' heights. As they do so, use the words *height* and *tall* as much as possible.

   Let's measure Luisa's *height*.

   She is 54 inches *tall*.

2. Help the students take turns weighing themselves on a small bathroom scale. As they do so, use the words *pounds* and *weigh* as much as possible.

   Let's see how much Nhat *weighs*.

   The scale says 58 *pounds*.

cavities, teeth, dentist

1. Pretend to have a toothache. Pantomime visiting the dentist (acted by a student).

   Oh my tooth hurts! I am going to see the dentist.

   Dr. Garcia, my tooth hurts so badly. See? It's this one.

2. Sketch a tooth on the board, making a dot in the middle of it. Tell the students that your tooth has a *cavity*. Go back to the student dentist, and pantomime having the tooth filled.

   Dr. Garcia, are you going to put a filling in my cavity?

3. Ask for a student volunteer to show a filling in his or her mouth. Explain that we can tell how many cavities people have had by counting their fillings.

Investigation 3

sleep, time

1. Write 10:00 P.M. on the board. Explain that this is the time you go to bed. Then pretend to be sleeping. After a few seconds, pretend to wake up. Write 6:00 A.M. on the board. Tell students that this is the time you get up.

2. Incorporate the word *sleep* into yes-or-no questions that challenge students to calculate how long you slept.

   Did I sleep for more than 2 hours?

   Did I sleep for less than 4 hours?

   Did I sleep for at least 6 hours?

3. Draw a simple clock on the board and have studdnts come up and draw the hands to show the *time* they go to bed and the *time* they get up.

Blackline Masters

_____ , 19 ____

Dear Family,

Our class has begun a new mathematics unit called *The Shape of the Data*. This unit is an introduction to collecting, representing, describing, and interpreting data. We are constantly bombarded with numerical information about everything around us—9 out of 10 doctors recommend brand X; the median age of the U.S. population is 32.9; in our country, 80% of the water is used for irrigation. This wealth of data can become confusing, or it can help us make choices about our actions.

In this unit, students will consider questions such as these: How many people are in a family? How much taller is a fourth grader than a first grader? They will be collecting their own numerical data, organizing it, representing it using graphs, and sharing their findings with the other students.

It can be easy for you to become involved in this unit, because your child may ask you questions as part of his or her data collection activities. Give your full attention to these questions and help your child record your answers, since they will be the basis of work in class.

For example, in one homework assignment, your child will look at some data our class has gathered. These data tell about the number of brothers and sisters each person in the class has. Your child will make a graph to show this information and then write brief statements about the "typical" number of brothers and sisters. Your child may want to collect similar data from adult friends and relatives and add that data to the graph.

You will find that there are many opportunities to collect data around your home. Which color or make of car is the most common on your street? Why might that be? Do more households in your neighborhood have a dog or a cat? After a while, collecting and thinking about data can become a habit that you and your child share.

Sincerely,

How Many Brothers and Sisters?

Make a line plot of the class data about brothers and sisters.

What do you think is the typical number of brothers and sisters for a student in your class?

_____

Why do you think that?

_____

_____

Heights of Two Fourth Grade Classes

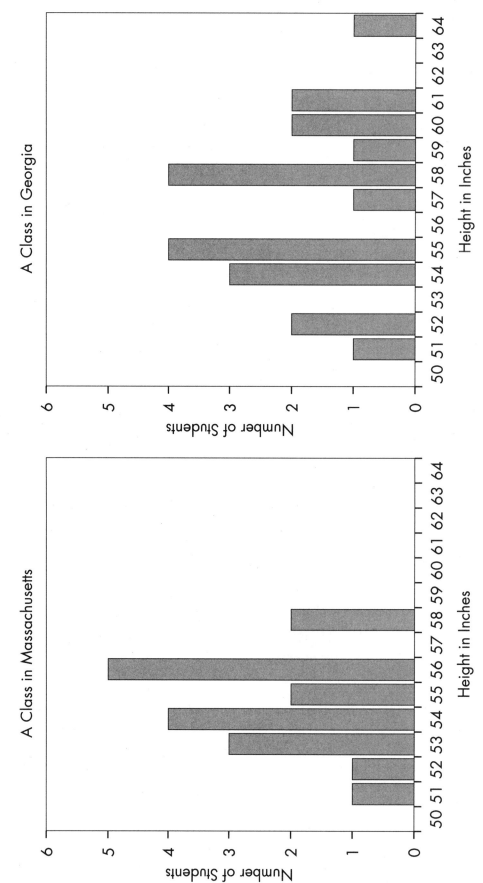

A Class in Massachusetts

A Class in Georgia

Number of Students

Height in Inches

How Tall Are Fourth Graders?

Make a quick sketch of the height data for your class. Try a different kind of sketch than you used in class.

Mystery Data A

The table and graph below show the same data.
These data represent some group of living things.
What do you think the group could be?
Give reasons for your answer.

Individual	Inches	Individual	Inches
A	78	M	80
B	75	N	72
C	81	O	78
D	82	P	73
E	82	Q	73
F	72	R	85
G	75	S	84
H	85	T	79
I	79	U	84
J	80	V	84
K	78	W	79
L	82	X	82

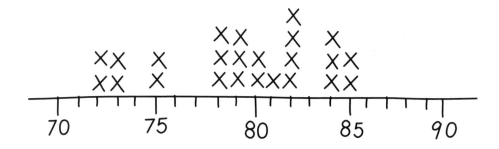

_____

_____

_____

_____

Mystery Data B

The table and graph below show the same data.
These data represent some group of living things.
What do you think the group could be?
Give reasons for your answer.

Individual	Inches	Individual	Inches
A	78	J	54
B	96	K	72
C	114	L	108
D	94	M	84
E	63	N	80
F	72	O	72
G	86	P	54
H	93	Q	79
I	64	R	116

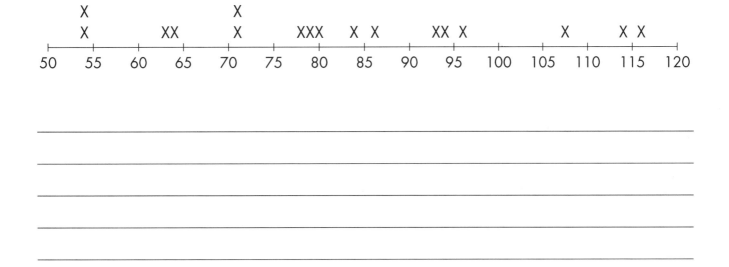

_____

_____

_____

_____

_____

_____

_____

Mystery Data C

This table and graph show the same data.
The data represent a group of living things.
What do you think the group might be?
Give reasons for your answer.

Individual	Inches	Individual	Inches
A	20	H	21
B	19.5	I	18
C	18.5	J	17
D	22	K	20
E	21.5	L	20.5
F	20	M	19.5
G	18	N	22

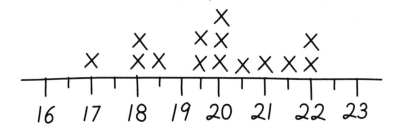

_____

_____

_____

_____

_____

_____

_____

_____

_____

Looking at Mystery Data

The table below shows some data about a group of living things.
Describe the data.
What do you think the living things might be?
Give reasons for your answer.

Individual	Inches	Individual	Inches
A	1932	G	4392
B	2592	H	2676
C	3624	I	1764
D	3336	J	2124
E	1956	K	3264
F	2628		

_____

_____

_____

_____

_____

_____

_____

_____

_____

_____

_____

_____

_____

How Many Cavities?

How many cavities have you had?

_____

How did you find out the number of cavities you
have had?

_____

_____

_____

Cat Weights

Organize these data about cats in a graph or plot.
What important landmarks do you see?
Describe what these data tell you about cats.

Name	Weight	Name	Weight
Ravena	14 pounds	Alexander	11 pounds
Lady Jane Grey	8.5 pounds	Lady	12 pounds
Peebles	9 pounds	Mittens	10.5 pounds
Grey Kitty	9 pounds	George	14.5 pounds
Weary	15 pounds	Pepper	12 pounds
Misty	9 pounds	Strawberry	14.5 pounds
Wally	10 pounds	K.C.	16 pounds
Amex	10 pounds	Charcoal	12 pounds
Melissa	11 pounds	Tigger	8 pounds
Oddfuzz	18 pounds	Tomonochi	8 pounds
Diva	11 pounds	Katenka	8.5 pounds
Peau de Soie	7 pounds	Harmony	12 pounds

_____

_____

_____

_____

_____

_____

Another Mystery

This graph shows some data about a group of living things. What do you think they are?

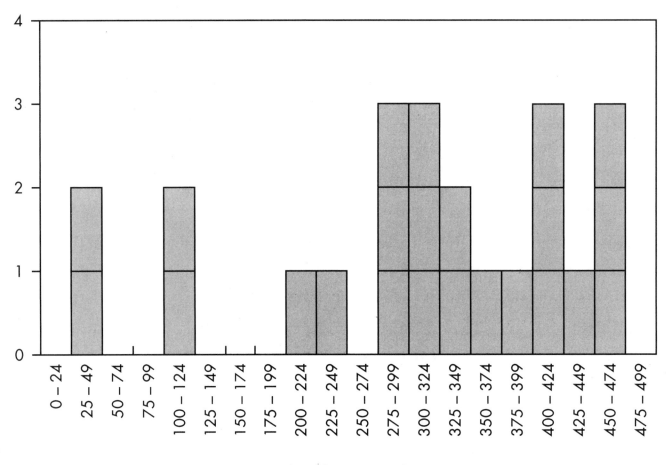

Weight in Pounds

_____

_____

_____

_____

_____

Cavity Data

These data are from a dentist in Massachusetts.
He counted the number of cavities in a group of
9- to 12-year-olds who visited his office.

What can you say about these data?
How does your class compare with this group?

```
X
X
X               X
X               X
X               X
X               X
X               X
X  X  X  X  X
X  X  X  X  X          X          X
0  1  2  3  4  5  6  7  8  9 10 11 12 13 14 15
```

_____

_____

_____

_____

_____

_____

_____

_____

_____

_____

'93 NBA ALL-STAR **Charles Barkley** Phoenix Suns 78"	'93 NBA ALL-STAR **Sean Elliott** San Antonio Spurs 80"
'93 NBA ALL-STAR **Shawn Kemp** Seattle SuperSonics 82"	'93 NBA ALL-STAR **Karl Malone** Utah Jazz 81"
'93 NBA ALL-STAR **Clyde Drexler** Portland Trail Blazers 79"	'93 NBA ALL-STAR **Tim Hardaway** Golden State Warriors 72"
'93 NBA ALL-STAR **Dan Majerle** Phoenix Suns 78"	'93 NBA ALL-STAR **Danny Manning** Los Angeles Clippers 82"

'93 NBA ALL-STAR	'93 NBA ALL-STAR
Hakeem Olajuwon Houston Rockets **84"**	**Brad Dougherty** Cleveland Cavaliers **84"**
'93 NBA ALL-STAR **Terry Porter** Portland Trail Blazers **75"**	'93 NBA ALL-STAR **Joe Dumars** Detroit Pistons **75"**
'93 NBA ALL-STAR **David Robinson** San Antonio Spurs **85"**	'93 NBA ALL-STAR **Patrick Ewing** New York Knicks **84"**
'93 NBA ALL-STAR **John Stockton** Utah Jazz **73"**	'93 NBA ALL-STAR **Larry Johnson** Charlotte Hornets **79"**

'93 NBA ALL-STAR	'93 NBA ALL-STAR
Michael Jordan Chicago Bulls **78"**	**Mark Price** Cleveland Cavaliers **72"**
Larry Nance Cleveland Cavaliers **82"**	**Isiah Thomas** Detroit Pistons **73"**
Shaquille O'Neal Orlando Magic **85"**	**Detlef Schrempf** Indiana Pacers **82"**
Scottie Pippen Chicago Bulls **79"**	**Dominique Wilkins** Atlanta Hawks **80"**

Three Nights' Sleep

How much sleep do you actually get?

Night 1
Amount of sleep:
Notes:

Night 2
Amount of sleep:
Notes:

Night 3
Amount of sleep:
Notes:

Wake Up!

How do you wake up when you have to?

_____

_____

Ask three people outside school how they wake up when they have to.

Name: Age: Method of waking up: Other important information:

Name: Age: Method of waking up: Other important information:

Name: Age: Method of waking up: Other important information:

Representing How People Wake Up

Organize and represent the data from Student Sheet 13 about methods people use to wake up when they have to. You may want to use color to highlight important parts of the data.

What do the data show?

_____

_____

What questions do you have about the data?

_____

_____

How Many Hours Do People Sleep?

Age	Females	Males
3–5	9.6	10.2
6–9	9.8	9.5
10–12	9.3	9.6
13–15	8.0	8.1
16–19	7.6	7.5
20–29	7.2	7.0
30–39	7.1	7.0
40–49	7.1	6.5
50–59	7.2	6.5
60–69	6.7	6.8
70–79	6.8	6.2

Source: Robert L. Williams, Ismet Karacan, and Carolyn J. Hursch, *Electroencephalography (EEG) of Human Sleep: Clinical Applications* (Wiley, 1974).

ONE-CENTIMETER GRAPH PAPER

91

Practice Pages

This optional section provides homework ideas for teachers who want or need to give more homework than is assigned to accompany the activities in this unit. The problems included here provide additional practice in learning about number relationships and in solving computation and number problems. For number units, you may want to use some of these if your students need more work in these areas or if you want to assign daily homework. For other units, you can use these problems so that students can continue to work on developing number and computation sense while they are focusing on other mathematical content in class. We recommend that you introduce activities in class before assigning related problems for homework.

Close to 100   This game is introduced in the unit *Mathematical Thinking at Grade 4*. If your students are familiar with the game, you can simply send home the directions, score sheet, and Numeral Cards so that students can play at home. If your students have not played the game before, introduce it in class and have students play once or twice before sending it home. For more challenge, students can try the variation listed at the bottom of the sheet. You might have students do this activity two times for homework in this unit.

Solving Problems in Two Ways   Solving problems in two ways is emphasized throughout the *Investigations* fourth grade curriculum. Here, we provide three sheets of problems that students solve in two different ways. Problems may be addition, subtraction, multiplication, or division. Students record each way they solved the problem. We recommend you give students an opportunity to share a variety of strategies for solving problems before you assign this homework.

Froggy Races   This type of problem is introduced in the unit *Landmarks in the Thousands*. Here, you are provided three problem sheets and one 300 chart, which you can copy for use with the problem sheets. You can also make up other problems in this format, using numbers that are appropriate for your students. On each sheet, students solve the problems and record their solution strategies.

How to Play Close to 100

Materials

- One deck of Numeral Cards
- Close to 100 Score Sheet for each player

Players: 1, 2, or 3

How to Play

1. Deal out six Numeral Cards to each player.

2. Use any four of your cards to make two numbers. For example, a 6 and a 5 could make either 56 or 65. Wild Cards can be used as any numeral. Try to make numbers that, when added, give you a total that is close to 100.

3. Write these two numbers and their total on the Close to 100 Score Sheet. For example: 42 + 56 = 98.

4. Find your score. Your score is the difference between your total and 100. For example, if your total is 98, your score is 2. If your total is 105, your score is 5.

5. Put the cards you used in a discard pile. Keep the two cards you didn't use for the next round.

6. For the next round, deal four new cards to each player. Make more numbers that come close to 100. When you run out of cards, mix up the discard pile and use them again.

7. Five rounds makes one game. Total your scores for the five rounds. LOWEST score wins!

Scoring Variation

Write the score with plus and minus signs to show the direction of your total away from 100. For example: If your total is 98, your score is –2. If your total is 105, your score is +5. The total of these two scores would be +3. Your goal is to get a total score for five rounds that is close to 0.

Close to 100 Score Sheet

Name_____

GAME 1   Score

Round 1:   _____ + _____ = _____   _____

Round 2:   _____ + _____ = _____   _____

Round 3:   _____ + _____ = _____   _____

Round 4:   _____ + _____ = _____   _____

Round 5:   _____ + _____ = _____   _____

                                    TOTAL SCORE   _____

Name_____

GAME 2   Score

Round 1:   _____ + _____ = _____   _____

Round 2:   _____ + _____ = _____   _____

Round 3:   _____ + _____ = _____   _____

Round 4:   _____ + _____ = _____   _____

Round 5:   _____ + _____ = _____   _____

                                    TOTAL SCORE   _____

0	0	1	1
0	0	1	1
2	2	3	3
2	2	3	3

96

4	4	5	5
4	4	5	5
<u>6</u>	<u>6</u>	7	7
<u>6</u>	<u>6</u>	7	7

Practice Page
The Shape of the Data

8	8	9	9
8	8	9	9
WILD CARD	WILD CARD		
WILD CARD	WILD CARD		

Practice Page A

Solve this problem in two different ways, and write about how you solved it:

26 + 90 =

Here is the first way I solved it:

Here is the second way I solved it:

Practice Page B

Solve this problem in two different ways, and write about how you solved it:

$$200 - 128 =$$

Here is the first way I solved it:

Here is the second way I solved it:

Practice Page C

Solve this problem in two different ways, and write about how you solved it:

13 × 8 =

Here is the first way I solved it:

Here is the second way I solved it:

300 CHART

1	2	3	4	5	6	7	8	9	10
11	12	13	14	15	16	17	18	19	20
21	22	23	24	25	26	27	28	29	30
31	32	33	34	35	36	37	38	39	40
41	42	43	44	45	46	47	48	49	50
51	52	53	54	55	56	57	58	59	60
61	62	63	64	65	66	67	68	69	70
71	72	73	74	75	76	77	78	79	80
81	82	83	84	85	86	87	88	89	90
91	92	93	94	95	96	97	98	99	100
101	102	103	104	105	106	107	108	109	110
111	112	113	114	115	116	117	118	119	120
121	122	123	124	125	126	127	128	129	130
131	132	133	134	135	136	137	138	139	140
141	142	143	144	145	146	147	148	149	150
151	152	153	154	155	156	157	158	159	160
161	162	163	164	165	166	167	168	169	170
171	172	173	174	175	176	177	178	179	180
181	182	183	184	185	186	187	188	189	190
191	192	193	194	195	196	197	198	199	200
201	202	203	204	205	206	207	208	209	210
211	212	213	214	215	216	217	218	219	220
221	222	223	224	225	226	227	228	229	230
231	232	233	234	235	236	237	238	239	240
241	242	243	244	245	246	247	248	249	250
251	252	253	254	255	256	257	258	259	260
261	262	263	264	265	266	267	268	269	270
271	272	273	274	275	276	277	278	279	280
281	282	283	284	285	286	287	288	289	290
291	292	293	294	295	296	297	298	299	300

Practice Page
The Shape of the Data

Practice Page D

Solve each problem. You may want to use a 300 chart to help.

1. Two frogs had a race. Freda Frog took 7 jumps of 25. Frances Frog took 3 jumps of 50. Who was ahead? How do you know?

2. In a second race, Freda took 15 jumps of 20. Frances took 7 jumps of 40. Who was ahead? How do you know?

3. In the last race, Freda decided to take jumps of 30. She took 6 jumps of 30. How many more jumps of 30 did she need to reach 300? How do you know?

Practice Page E

Solve each problem. You may want to use a 300 chart to help.

1. Two frogs had a race. Foona Frog took 4 jumps of 50. Feema Frog took 9 jumps of 25. Who was ahead? How do you know?

2. In a second race, Foona took 20 jumps of 15. Feema took 40 jumps of 7. Who was ahead? How do you know?

3. In the last race, Foona decided to take jumps of 10. She took 18 jumps of 10. How many more jumps of 10 did she need to reach 300? How do you know?

Practice Page F

Solve each problem. You may want to use a 300 chart to help.

1. Two frogs had a race. Flip Frog took 20 jumps of 11. Flop Frog took 5 jumps of 40. Who was ahead? How do you know?

2. In a second race, Flip took 15 jumps of 15. Flop took 8 jumps of 30. Who was ahead? How do you know?

3. In the last race, Flip decided to take jumps of 60. He took 2 jumps of 60. How many more jumps of 60 did he need to reach 300? How do you know?